Dig It!

Written by Lockwood DeWitt
Illustrated by B. K. Hixson

Dig It!

Copyright © 2003
First Printing • March 2003
B. K. Hixson

Published by Loose in the Lab, Inc.
9462 South 560 West
Sandy, Utah 84070

www.looseinthelab.com

Library of Congress Cataloging-in-Publication Data:

Hixson, B. K.
    Dig It! / Lockwood DeWitt, B. K. Hixson
    p.   cm.-(Loose in the Lab Science Series)

    Includes index
    ISBN 0-931801-02-9
   1. Geology experiments–juvenile literature. [1. Geology experiments 2. Experiments] I. Lockwood DeWitt
II. B. K. Hixson III. Loose in the Lab IV. Title V. Series
QP550.1   2003
152.14

Printed in the United States of America
Rock On!

Dedication

*"I really think that your mom would like this in the front yard.
Let's see if we can tie it to the roof of the truck."*

K. L. Hixson

Here's to our dad, grandpa, and husband, who loved to be
outdoors and sit in the dirt. Dad was ready at the drop of a hat for any
fossil- or rock-collecting adventure that would take him up to the
plateaus of Southern Utah for Moqui marbles, to the edge of the vast
volcanic deserts in Oregon for pumice and obsidian, or high up into
Wyoming so that he could stand on the edge of the Green River
Formation and fish for 50 million-year-old fossils. And, of course, there
was the petrified tree that dad wanted to bring home from Arizona.
Fortunately, we weren't driving a flatbed.

We thoroughly enjoyed the time we got to spend together on
this old, blue sphere and look forward to many more adventures when
we hook up again for the next skip across a planet somewhere in the
universe. Hugs and kisses from all of us!

Acknowledgments

My earliest geology memories are simply stories that my folks told me about visiting Yellowstone as a newborn and having the pleasure of getting my buns dunked in the run-off from the hot pools feeding the Firehole River. Add to that numerous trips to Glacier, fossil hunting in the Little Belt Mountains, and digging layers of colorful mica out of the river rock lining the Missouri, and you have a pretty formative set of experiences before you hit first grade. I have fond memories of exploring old, abandoned mines in Colorado, being given guided tours of the Cascades and Sierra Nevada Mountain Ranges by my college pal, Andy Mills, and zipping out to Death Valley and Joshua Tree to explore the incredible layers of rock both by myself and with 150 fifth graders in tow. Trips all over Utah with my pop and our annual visit to the Tucson Rock and Gem Show pretty much have rounded out my experiences—but I am hoping we are ages from the finish line.

As for my educational outlook, the hands-on perspective, and the use of humor in the classroom, Dr. Fox, my senior professor at Oregon State University, gets the credit for shaping my educational philosophy while simultaneously recognizing that even at the collegiate level we were on to something a little different. He did his very best to encourage, nurture, and support me while I was getting basketloads of opposition for being willing to swim upstream. There were also several colleagues who helped to channel my enthusiasm during those early, formative years of teaching: Dick Bishop, Dick Hinton, Dee Strange, Connie Ridgway, and Linda Zimmermann. Thanks for your patience, friendship, and support.

Next up are all the folks who get to do the dirty work that makes the final publication look so polished but very rarely get the credit they deserve. Our resident graphics guru, Kris Barton, gets a nod for scanning and cleaning the artwork you find on these pages, as well as putting together the graphics that make up the cover. A warm Yankee yahoo to Eve Laubner, our editor, who passes her comments on so that Kathleen Hixson and Eve Laubner can take turns simultaneously proofreading the text while mocking my writing skills.

Once we have a finished product, it has to be printed by the good folks back east, so that Gary Facente, Louisa Walker, Selina Gerow, and the Delta Education gang can market and ship the books, collect the money, and send us a couple of nickels.

Mom and Dad, as always, get the end credits. Thanks for the education, encouragement, and love. And for Kathy and the kids—Porter, Shelby, Courtney, and Aubrey—all my hugs and kisses.

Repro Rights

There is very little about this book that is truly formal, but at the insistence of our wise and esteemed counsel, let us declare: *No part of this book may be reproduced or utilized in any form or by any means, electronic or mechanical, including photocopying, recording, or by any information storage and retrieval system, without permission in writing from the publisher.* That's us.

More Legal Stuff

Official disclaimer for you aspiring scientists and lab groupies. This is a hands-on science book. By the very intent of its design, you will be directed to use common, nontoxic, household items in a safe and responsible manner to avoid injury to yourself and others who are present while you are pursuing your quest for knowledge and enlightenment in the world of geology. Just make sure that you have a fire blanket handy and a wall-mounted video camera to corroborate your story.

If, for some reason, perhaps even beyond your own control, you have an affinity for disaster, we wish you well. *But we in no way take any responsibility for any injury that is incurred to any person using the information provided in this book or for any damage to personal property or effects that is directly or indirectly a result of the suggested activities contained herein.* Translation: You're on your own, despite the fact that many have preceded you in the lab. Don't eat any of the rocks, and remember that minerals are only good if in a chelated form (that's another book altogether), and snorting most of the chemicals suggested in this book will do nothing to improve your disposition.

Less Formal Legal Stuff

If you happen to be a home schooler or very enthusiastic school teacher, please feel free to make copies of this book for your classroom or personal family use—one copy per student, up to 35 students. If you would like to use an experiment from this book for a presentation to your faculty or school district, we would be happy to oblige. Just give us a whistle and we will send you a release for the particular lab activity you wish to use. Please contact us at the address below. Thanks.

Special Requests
Loose in the Lab, Inc.
9462 South 560 West
Sandy, Utah 84070

Table of Contents

The National Content Standards (Grades K–4)

Earth materials are solid rocks and soils, water, and the gases of the atmosphere. The varied materials have different physical and chemical properties, which make them useful in different ways, for example, as building materials, as sources of fuel, or for growing the plants we use as food. Earth materials provide many of the resources that humans use.

The National Content Standards (Grades 5-8)

Some changes in the solid Earth can be described as the rock cycle. Old rocks at the Earth's surface weather, forming sediments that are buried, then compacted, heated, and often recrystallized into new rock. Eventually, those new rocks may be brought to the surface by the forces that drive plate motions, and the rock cycle continues.

The 10 Big Ideas About Geology & Corresponding Labs

1. Minerals are naturally occurring inorganic solids made of a single kind of material. These compounds are all crystalline, and their atoms are arranged in a regular, repeating pattern that is as much a part of the mineral's properties as its composition.

2. Minerals are the building blocks of all rocks. Every rock is made of at least one mineral, but more often two or more that have combined under conditions that allow for rock formation.

3. Minerals can form from gases (sublimation), liquids (precipitation), and solids (recrystallization).

4. Each mineral has a unique set of properties and can be identified using a series of standardized tests.

Table of Contents

5. Extrusive igneous rocks are formed when molten rock, called lava, erupts from a volcano onto the surface of the Earth and solidifies. One way that this happens is that volcanos erupt and expel molten lava. There are also cracks in the crust of the Earth that open up and ooze lava over hundreds of square miles.

6. Intrusive igneous rocks are formed when molten rock, called magma, cools and solidifies slowly under the Earth's surface.

7. Organic sedimentary rocks are formed when living matter dies, piles up, and then is compressed into rock.

8. Chemical sedimentary rocks are formed when minerals dissolved in water crystallize out, or precipitate, from solution.

9. Clastic sedimentary rocks are formed from weathered and eroded pieces of previously existing rocks that got deposited together and smooshed and cemented into rock.

Even More Contents

10. Metamorphic rocks started out as one kind of rock—igneous, sedimentary, or metamorphic—but got squished, heated, and changed into new rocks.

Science Fair Planner

Who Are You ? And ...

First of all, we may have an emergency at hand and we'll both want to cut to the chase and get the patient into the cardiac unit if necessary. So, before we go too much further, **define yourself**. Please check one and only one choice listed below and then immediately follow the directions that follow *in italics*. Thank you in advance for your cooperation.

I am holding this book because. . .

___ **A. I am a responsible, but panicked, parent.** My son / daughter / triplets (circle one) just informed me that his / her / their science fair project is due tomorrow. This is the only therapy I could afford on such short notice. This means that, if I were not holding this book, my hands would be encircling the soon-to-be-worm-bait's neck.

Directions: Can't say this is the first or the last time we heard that one. Hang in there, we can do this.

1. Quickly read the Table of Contents with the worm bait. The Big Ideas define what each section is about. Obviously, the kid is not passionate about science, or you would not be in this situation. See if you can find an idea that causes some portion of an eyelid or facial muscle to twitch.

If that does not work, we recommend narrowing the list to the following labs because they are fast, use materials that can be acquired with limited notice, and the intrinsic level of interest is generally quite high.

Lab #3 • Crystal Patterns • page 33
Lab #6 • Caffeine Cathedrals • page 51
Lab #8 • Silica Crystal Garden • page 57
Lab #14 • Mohs' Hardness Test • page 82
Lab #21 • Styrofoam Rock • page 114
Lab #33 • Distilled Fossils • page 169

How to Use This Book

2. *Take the materials list from the lab write-up and from page 253 of the Science Fair Project section and go shopping.*

3. *Assemble the materials and perform the lab at least once. Gather as much data as you can.*

4. *Go to page 253 and read the materials list. Then start on Step 1 of Preparing Your Science Fair Project. With any luck, you can dodge an academic disaster.*

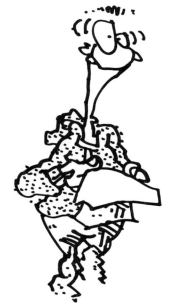

___ **B. I am worm bait.** My science fair project is due tomorrow, and there is not anything moldy in the fridge. I need a big Band-Aid in a hurry.

Directions: Same as Option A. You can decide if and when you want to clue your folks in on your current dilemma.

___ **C. I am the parent of a student who informed me that he/ she has been assigned a science fair project due in six to eight weeks.** My son/daughter has expressed an interest in science books with humorous illustrations that attempt to explain geology and associated phenomena.

Who Are You ? And ...

Directions: Well, you came to the right place. Give your kid these directions and stand back.

1. The first step is to read through the Table of Contents and see if anything grabs your interest. Read through several experiments, see if the science teacher has any of the more difficult-to-acquire materials like geology and mineral specimens, erosion screens, and some of the chemicals, and ask if they can be borrowed. Play with the experiments and see which one really tickles your fancy.

2. After you have found and conducted an experiment that you like, take a peek at the Science Fair Ideas and see if you would like to investigate one of those or create an idea of your own. The guidelines for those are listed in the Science Fair section. You have plenty of time so you can fiddle and fool with the original experiment and its derivations several times. Work until you have an original question you want to answer and then start the process. You are well on your way to an excellent grade.

___ D. I am a responsible student and have been assigned a science fair project due in six to eight weeks. I am interested in geology, and despite demonstrating maturity and wisdom well beyond the scope of my peers, I too still have a sense of humor. Enlighten and entertain me.

Directions: Cool. Being teachers, we have heard reports of this kind of thing happening but usually in an obscure and hard-to-locate town several states removed. Nonetheless, congratulations.

Same as Option C. You have plenty of time and should be able to score very well. We'll keep our eyes peeled when the Nobel Prizes are announced in a couple of decades.

How to Use This Book

___ **E. I am a parent who home schools my child/children.** I am always on the lookout for high-quality curriculum materials that are not only educationally sound but also kid- and teacher-friendly. I am not particularly strong in science, but I realize it is a very important topic. How is this book going to help me out?

Directions: In a lot of ways we created this book specifically for home schoolers.

1. We have taken the National Content Standards, the guidelines that are used by all public and private schools nationwide to establish their curriculum base, and listed them in the Table of Contents. You now know where you stand with respect to the national standards.

2. We then break these standards down and list the major ideas that you should want your kid to know. We call these the Big Ideas. Some people call them objectives, others call them curriculum standards, educational benchmarks, or assessment norms. Same apple, different name. The bottom line is that when your children are done studying this unit on geology, you want them not only to understand and explain each of the Big Ideas listed in this book, but also, to be able to defend and argue their position based on experiential evidence that they have collected.

3. Building on the Big Ideas, we have collected and rewritten over 40 hands-on science labs. Each one has been specifically selected so that it supports the Big Idea that it is correlated to. This is critical. As the kids do the science experiment, they see, smell, touch, and hear the experiment. They will store that information in several places in their brains. When it comes time to comprehend the Big Idea, the concrete hands-on experiences provide the foundation for building the Idea, which is quite often abstract. Kids who merely read about shield volcanos, popcorn rhyolite bombs, and soil layers, or who see pictures of rocks, minerals, and soils but have never squeezed them between their fingers are trying to build abstract ideas on abstract ideas and quite often miss the mark.

Who Are You ? And ...

For example: I can show you a recipe in a book for chocolate chip cookies and ask you to reiterate it. Or I can turn you loose in a kitchen, have you mix the ingredients, grease the pan, plop the dough on the cookie sheet, slide everything into the oven, and wait impatiently until they pop out eight minutes later. Chances are that the description given by the person who actually made the cookies is going to be much clearer because it is based on their true understanding of the process, **because it is based on experience.**

4. *Once you have completed the experiment, there are a number of extension ideas under the Science Fair Extensions that allow you to spend as much or as little time on the ideas as you deem necessary.*

5. *A word about humor. Science is not usually known for being funny even though* Bill Nye, The Science Guy, *Beaker from* Sesame Street, *and* Beakman's World *do their best to mingle the two. That's all fine and dandy, but we want you to know that we incorporate humor because it is scientifically (and educationally) sound to do so. Plus it's really at the root of our personalities. Here's what we know:*

When we laugh ...
a. Our pupils dilate, increasing the amount of light entering the eye.
b. Our heart rate increases, which pumps more blood to the brain.
c. Oxygen-rich blood to the brain means the brain is able to collect, process, and store more information. Big I.E.: increased comprehension.
d. Laughter relaxes muscles, which can be involuntarily tense if a student is uncomfortable or fearful of an academic topic.
e. Laughter stimulates the immune system, which will ultimately translate into overall health and fewer kids who say they are sick of science.
f. Socially, it provides an acceptable pause in the academic routine, which then gives the student time to regroup and prepare to address some of the more difficult ideas with a renewed spirit. They can study longer and focus on ideas more efficiently.
g. Laughter releases chemicals in the brain that are associated with pleasure and joy.

6. *If you follow the book in the order in which it is written, you will be able to build ideas and concepts in a logical and sequential pattern. But that is by no means necessary. For a complete set of guidelines on our ideas on how to teach home-schooled kids science, check out our book,* Why's the Cat on Fire? How to Excel at Teaching Science to Your Home-Schooled Kids.

How to Use This Book

___ **F. I am a public/private school teacher,** and this looks like an interesting book to add ideas to my classroom lesson plans.

Directions: It is, and please feel free to do so. However, while this is a great classroom resource for kids, may we also recommend several other titles: Fire on the Mountain *(Basic Intro to Volcanos),* The Rock Cycle Blues *(The Rock Cycle),* Mohs' Mineral Menagerie, *(Minerals, Crystals, and Ores),* Tectonic Puzzles *(Physical Geology and Landforms),* Trilobites to Mammoth Tusks *(Fossils and the Fossil History of the Earth),* **and** Strike, Dip, and Eureka! *(Stratigraphy, Mapping, and Resource Geology).*

These books have teacher-preparation pages, student-response sheets or lab pages, lesson plans, bulletin board ideas, discovery center ideas, vocabulary sheets, unit pretests, unit exams, lab practical exams, and student grading sheets. Basically everything you need if you are a science nincompoop, and a couple of cool ideas if you are a seasoned veteran with an established curriculum. All of the ideas that are covered in this one book are covered much more thoroughly in the others that we listed. They were specifically written for teachers.

___ **G. My son/daughter/grandson/niece/father-in-law** is interested in science, and this looks like fun.

Directions: Congratulations on your selection. Add a gift certificate to the local rock store and a guidebook to mineral deposits in your state and you have the perfect Saturday afternoon field trip.

___ **H. My kennel club is concerned about presenting a well-rounded collection of breeds at the next dog show. We can't seem to find a rock hound anywhere. Can you help?**

Directions: Nope. Too busy unloading this box of leaverite.

Lab Safety

Contained herein are 40+ science activities to help you better understand the nature and characteristics of geology and geological processes as we currently understand these things. However, because you are on your own in this journey, we thought it prudent to share some basic wisdom and experience in the safety department.

Read the Instructions

An interesting concept, especially if you are a teenager. Take a minute before you jump in and get going to read all of the instructions as well as warnings. If you do not understand something, stop and ask an adult for help.

Clean Up All Messes

Keep your lab area clean. It will make it easier to put everything away at the end and may also prevent contamination and the subsequent germination of a species of mutant tomato bug larva. You will also find that chemicals perform with more predictability if they are not poisoned with foreign molecules.

Organize

Translation: Put it back where you get it. If you need any more clarification, there is an opening at the landfill for you.

HELLO.

GOODBYE.

Dispose of Poisons Properly

This will not be much of a problem with the labs that are suggested in this book. However, if you happen to wander over into one of the many disciplines that incorporates the use of more advanced chemicals, then we would suggest that you use great caution with the materials and definitely dispose of any and all poisons properly.

Practice Good Fire Safety

If there is a fire in the room, notify an adult immediately. If an adult is not in the room and the fire is manageable, smother the outbreak with a fire blanket or use a fire extinguisher. When the fire is contained, immediately send someone to find an adult. If, for any reason, you happen to catch on fire, **REMEMBER: Stop, Drop, and Roll.** Never run; it adds oxygen to the fire, making it burn faster, and it also scares the bat guano out of the neighbors when they see the neighbor kids running down the block doing an imitation of a campfire marshmallow without the stick.

Protect Your Skin

It is a good idea to always wear protective gloves whenever you are working with chemicals. Again, this particular book does not suggest or incorporate hazardous chemicals in its lab activities. If you do happen to spill a chemical on your skin, notify an adult immediately and then flush the area with water for 15 minutes. It's unlikely, but if irritation develops, have your parents or another responsible adult look at it. If it appears to be of concern, contact a physician. Take any information that you have about the chemical with you.

Lab Safety

Save Your Nose Hairs

Sounds like a cause celebre L.A. style, but it is really good advice. To smell a chemical to identify it, hold the open container six to ten inches down and away from your nose. Make a clockwise circular motion with your hand over the opening of the container, "wafting" some of the fumes toward your nose. This will allow you to safely smell some of the fumes without exposing yourself to a large dose of anything noxious. This technique may help prevent a nosebleed or your lungs from accidentally getting burned by chemicals.

Wear Goggles If Appropriate

If the lab asks you to heat or mix chemicals, be sure to wear protective eyewear. Also have an eyewash station or running water available. You never know when something is going to splatter, splash, or react unexpectedly. It is better to look like a nerd and be prepared than to schedule a trip down to pick out a Seeing Eye™ dog. If you do happen to accidentally get chemicals into your eye, flush the area for 15 minutes. If any irritation or pain develops, immediately go see a doctor.

Lose the Comedy Routine

You should have plenty of time scheduled during your day to mess around, but science lab is not one of them. Horseplay breaks glassware, spills chemicals, and creates unnecessary messes—things that parents do not appreciate. Trust us on this one.

No Eating

Do not eat while performing a lab. Putting your food in the lab area contaminates your food and the experiment. This makes for bad science and worse indigestion. Avoid poisoning yourself and goobering up your labware by observing this rule.

Happy and safe experimenting!

Dig It! • Lockwood DeWitt & B. K. Hixson

Recommended Materials Suppliers

For every lesson in this book, we offer a list of materials. Many of these are very easy to acquire, and if you do not have them in your home already, you will be able to find them at the local grocery or hardware store. For more difficult items, we have selected for your convenience a small but respectable list of suppliers who will meet your needs in a timely and economical manner. Call for a catalog or quote on the item that you are looking for, and they will be happy to give you a hand.

Loose in the Lab
9462 South 560 West
Sandy, UT 84070
Phone 1-888-403-1189
Fax 1-801-568-9586
www.looseinthelab.com

Delta Education
80 NW Boulevard
Nashua, NH 03063
Phone 1-800-442-5444
Fax 1-800-282-9560
www.delta-education.com

Hubbard Scientific
401 W Hickory Street
Fort Collins, CO 80522
Phone 1-800-289-9299
Fax 1-970-484-1198
www.shnta.com

Ward's Scientific
5100 W Henrietta Road
Rochester, NY 14692
Phone 1-800-387-7822
Fax 1-716-334-6174
www.wardsci.com

Educational Innovations
151 River Road
Cos Cob, CT 06807
Phone 1-888-912-7474
Fax 1-203-629-2739
www.teachersource.com

Frey Scientific
100 Paragon Parkway
Mansfield, OH 44903
Phone 1-800-225-FREY
Fax 1-419-589-1546
www.freyscientific.com

Your Local Rock Shop
(See the Yellow Pages.)

Check for Rock Clubs.

Top Gem Minerals
1248 N Main Street
Tucson, AZ 85703
Phone 1-520-622-6633
Fax 1-520-792-2978
www.topgem.com

The Ideas,
Lab Activities,
& Science Fair
Extensions

Big Idea 1

Minerals are naturally occurring inorganic solids made of a single kind of material. These compounds are all crystalline, and their atoms are arranged in a regular, repeating pattern that is as much a part of the mineral's properties as its composition.

Mineral Q & A

What is a Mineral?

A **mineral** is an **inorganic, crystalline, chemical substance that occurs naturally.** Rock salt that forms on the surface of dry lakes is a mineral called halite. Pyrite, or fool's gold, found in riverbeds is also a mineral. The characteristic that separates minerals from other naturally occurring substances is that they are completely **uniform in composition.** They are made of a single chemical substance through and through, nothing else.

What is a Crystal?

Crystals are **minerals made of a single chemical with linkages that repeat in a predictable pattern.** A crystal of fool's gold is made of billions of iron sulfide molecules stacked on top of one another in a regular pattern, forming cubes. Halite is nothing more than billions of cubes of sodium chloride, stacked and hooked together. The catch here is that not all crystals are large enough for you to see with your naked eye. It is very important to remember that not all minerals are crystalline.

How Many Minerals are There?

At last count, about 3,000 minerals had been identified. However, the search isn't over. It is likely that several new minerals will be found and identified in your lifetime alone.

How are Minerals Classified?

Every mineral has a unique chemical composition and crystal structure. Therefore, every mineral has its own set of unique properties. Just as you can be identified by the color of your eyes, your gender, your height, weight, and other characteristics, minerals are separated and identified by *their* individual characteristics.

Several tests can be performed to identify minerals. You will learn 8 of them, which will be covered in a little bit. In addition, minerals can also be separated and identified by chemical composition, optical characteristics like refraction and response to UV light, and crystal systems. Those are all a bit tricky, so we will save them for when you advance up the mineralogy trail.

Where are Minerals Found?

Wherever rocks are found, minerals are also found. Minerals worth collecting are found in places where the past conditions have led to the growth of large, nicely-colored and well-formed crystals. Once these crystals are formed, they are then exposed at or near the surface of the Earth by one of several processes.

How are Minerals Formed?

Good question. Proceed directly to the next several labs and take careful notes.

Sugar or Salt?

Geologically Speaking...

We start with minerals because they are the building blocks of all rocks. By definition, a mineral is a unique substance with unique properties. A rock is made up of two or more minerals, so in order to understand rocks, we start with minerals.

And, to start with minerals we are going to start with two very simple compounds, salt and sugar, and take a peek at the crystals that they form.

Once you get the hang of looking at crystal structure, we will move over to real minerals and use this information to help with identification.

Materials

1   Packet of salt
1   Packet of sugar
1   Hand lens
1   White pencil
1   Piece of black paper

Procedure

1. Empty the salt packet out onto a piece of black paper or any surface that will provide contrast between itself and the white salt crystals. In the first box on the next page, draw the crystals as you see them, and describe the crystals to the best of your ability.

2. Empty the sugar packet out onto a dark surface, just as you did with the salt. In the bottom space below, draw the crystals as you see them, and once again, describe the crystals.

Data & Observations

1. Salt

_____

_____

_____

_____

_____

_____

2. Sugar

_____

_____

_____

_____

_____

_____

Sugar or Salt?

How Come, Huh?

One of the characteristics that allows mineralogists and geologists to identify different kinds of minerals is the crystal structure of the specimen that they are examining.

In this case, the salt has a cubic crystal shape and, when you look at it under a microscope or hand lens, it appears to look like a pile of little boxes. The sugar has an appearance that is somewhat irregular. This is typical of larger, more complex molecules. Salt is sodium chloride, which stacks neatly into a cube. Sugar is a long hydrocarbon that tends to bend, wiggle, and not stack up as nicely as its seasoning counterpart.

Science Fair Extensions

1. Examine and compare other crystals to the salt and sugar crystals. Chemicals that are easy to find in the local grocery store are calcium chloride (snow melter), magnesium sulfate (epsom salts), and aluminum sulfate (alum).

2. Head to a rock shop or local museum of natural history and waddle into their gem and mineral section. Look at the different specimens. If you want to skip ahead to the crystal structure section, you can find and compare orthorhombic with tetragonal and triclinic crystal patterns. Or, you could just lean over the case and sigh, *ooh aah*, like we do.

Geodes on the Halfshell

Geologically Speaking ...

By definition, a geode is a deposit of mineral matter that has crystallized in a pocket. The outside of most geodes, called the rind, is usually a dark material that is very ugly, but the inside can range from plain and geologically homely to quite beautiful.

A plastic eggshell is going to be used to simulate the gas pockets that are found in some lava flows. Copper sulfate crystals in solution will represent minerals dissolved in ground water. This "ground water" will then be added to your eggshell. When the water evaporates, a genuine, simulated geode lined with beautiful robin's egg blue crystals will remain. Guaranteed better than dimestore jewelry!

Materials

1   Bottle of copper sulfate crystals
    Hot water
1   Plastic cup, 12 oz.
4   Eggshell halves, empty and clean
        or
2   Plastic eggshells
1   Eggshell carton
1   Spoon, plastic
1   Hand lens

Procedure

1. Fill the plastic cup two-thirds full with hot water. Pour a spoonful of copper sulfate into the cup. Stir these crystals with the spoon until they all dissolve. Add a little more copper sulfate and continue stirring. When you get to the point where no more copper crystals will dissolve, you have made a saturated solution.

Geodes on the Halfshell

2. Open up two plastic eggs or pre-pare four clean eggshells and set them up-right in an empty egg carton.

3. Fill each of the eggshells with the copper sulfate solution that you have made. Carefully set the eggshells aside, and ob-serve what happens as the solution evapo-rates over several days.

4. When the solution has completely evaporated, you will have a batch of home-made geodes—and in a fraction of the time it takes for the real things to be produced.

Data & Observations

Examine your eggshells each day for four consecutive days. Select one eggshell and record your observations over the four days by drawing the inside of the eggshell in the spaces provided.

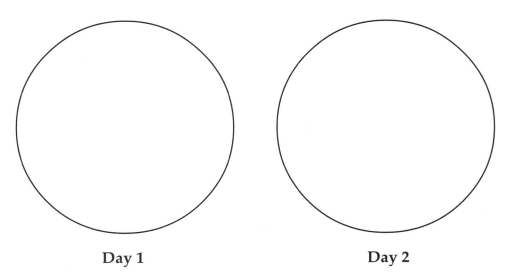

Day 1   **Day 2**

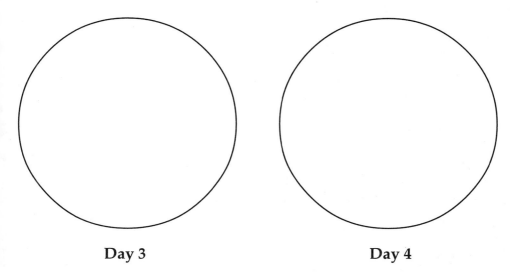

Day 3   Day 4

How Come, Huh?

Geodes can form in many ways and may contain many different kinds of minerals. Many types of geodes have their own specific names. For example, those that form in rhyolite flows and are completely filled with banded agate are called thunder eggs. These are Oregon's State Rock.

Limestone caverns could be thought of as extremely large geodes. There is a big, empty space with mineral deposits growing on the rock. It fits our loose definition. Go hike a geode!

Science Fair Extensions

3. The size of the crystals is dependent upon a couple of factors, including how fast the solution cools. Design and carry out an experiment where you show how the rate of cooling affects crystal size.

4. Make geodes using other kinds of chemicals. All of the sulfates—magnesium, nickel, and potassium—are fun.

Geodes on the Halfshell

Geo Profile: Geodes

The word "Geode" can be a little confusing, but generally speaking, a geode is a hollow or empty space in rock, partly filled with crystals that are clearly different from the surrounding rock. People typically think of geodes as having some empty space left, so the mineral crystals are free-standing, not just a solid mass.

Geodes start the process of formation as an empty space in a rock. This void space may be a gas bubble in a lava flow, a hole dissolved out in a bed of limestone or dolomite, or any other empty space. On occasion, for example, a shell might not fill in with sediment completely when it's buried and fossilized. This creates the type of void space that is needed for geodes to form.

As ground water works through rock, it dissolves minerals. If the mineral concentration becomes high enough, the water may drop part of its dissolved minerals where there is open space. This process is called precipitation. (See Big Idea 3.) The two most common minerals to be deposited this way are calcite and quartz, but many minerals can form in geodes. It is not uncommon to have two or more minerals in a single geode. Frequently (but not always) the rock right around the hole is different from the host rock. This outer ring is called the "rind." Geologic terminology is full of surprises. The inner minerals may show delicate and perfect crystal form, weird colors, strange patterns or banding, or combinations of these features. Geodes can range in size from a fraction of an inch to many feet across.

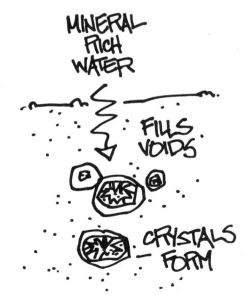

Crystal Patterns

Geologically Speaking ...

Part of the Big Idea in this section is that minerals are crystalline; that is, their atoms are arranged in regular, repeating patterns. This repetition can get a lot like math, and we want to avoid that here. But mathematically, all the different patterns of repetition can be grouped into six general patterns, so all the different forms taken by minerals can be grouped into these seven classes: Isometric, Tetragonal, Orthorhombic, Hexagonal, Trigonal, Triclinic, and Monoclinic.

Recognition of symmetry is important to recognizing the mineral groups, so it would be a good idea to talk about it for a moment here. Symmetry can be thought of in terms of operations that you can carry out that don't change the appearance of something. For example, if you have a perfect cube, you can't tell one face from another. Turn the cube one-quarter of a turn and you (theoretically) won't be able to tell you've turned it. Turn it a half turn or three-quarters of a turn and you still won't be able to tell that anything has changed. This is called rotational symmetry.

Another kind of symmetry involves the mirror plane. For many objects, one side is just like the other. Most familiar animals basically have a mirror plane of symmetry. Imagine a mirror that runs from top to bottom along your body. The reflection on the mirror would look like the other side of your body. Your left hand is a reflection of your right hand, and so on.

So the mineral forms are grouped by the kinds of symmetry operations you can carry out on them. The most symmetrical form is a sphere, but minerals can't crystallize into spheres. The most *symmetrical mineral form* is the cube. Consider the picture at the right.

Crystal Patterns

Materials

1	Pair of scissors
1	Bottle of glue
1	Copier
10	Sheets of paper

Procedure

1. Find a copier at a local copy shop or in the school secretary's office. If all else fails, use the copier that your mom has stashed in the knife drawer. (It may look suspiciously like a pencil.) Make one copy of each of the six crystal patterns on pages 36 through 41. If you use construction paper, your designs will hold up better and will certainly be more colorful.

2. Cut each of the patterns out and, folding and gluing in the appropriate places, recreate each of the six crystal patterns you see on the next page.

How Come, Huh?

Symmetry is very important to crystal identification but it is really a topic that you should save for later in life. These books are intended for kids who, at best, are wading through high school. We will leave the heavy-duty mineralogy for your college days.

Science Fair Extensions

5. There are other patterns that can be made from paper. When I was in fifth grade, one of my accomplishments of note was creating dodecahedrons to hang from the ceiling in Mr. Goffard's classroom. Find a good book on origami and start wrestling.

Dig It! • Lockwood DeWitt & B. K. Hixson

Crystal Forms

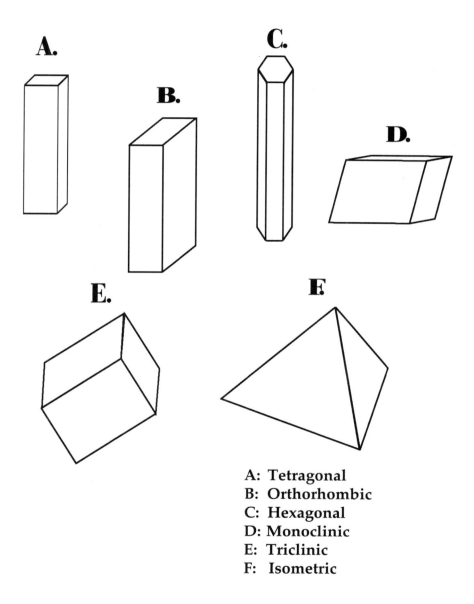

A: Tetragonal
B: Orthorhombic
C: Hexagonal
D: Monoclinic
E: Triclinic
F: Isometric

Tetragonal

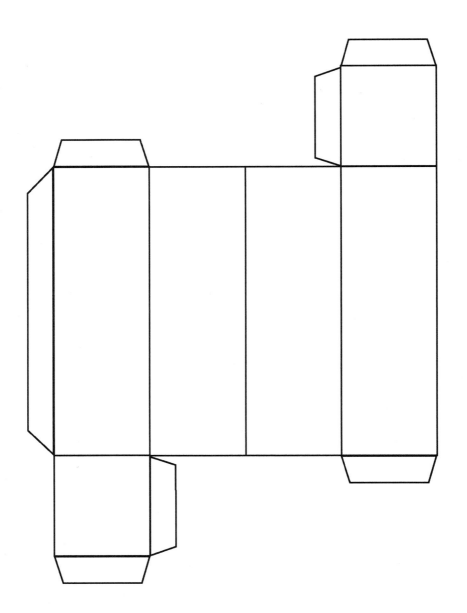

Dig It! • Lockwood DeWitt & B. K. Hixson

Orthorhombic

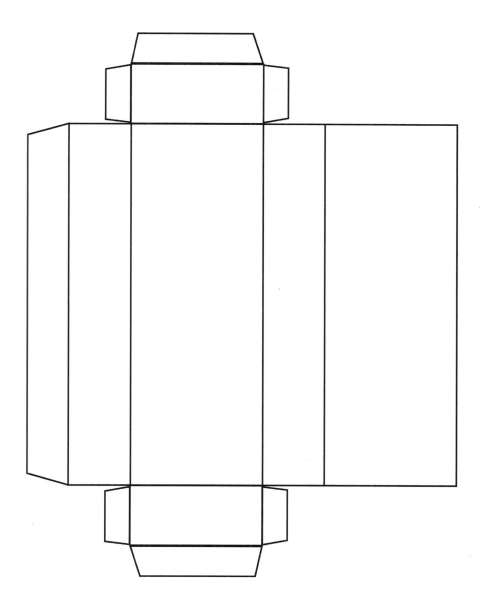

Hexagonal

Monoclinic

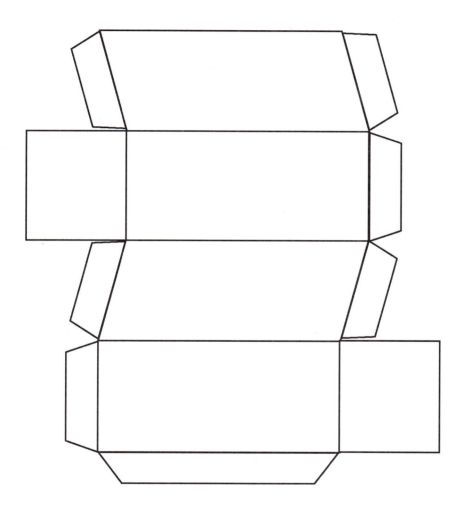

Triclinic

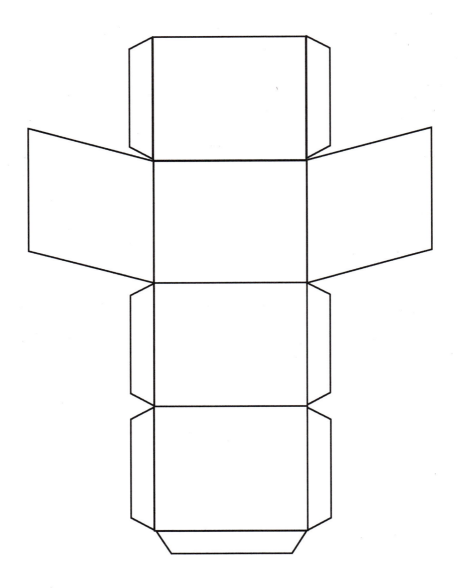

Isometric

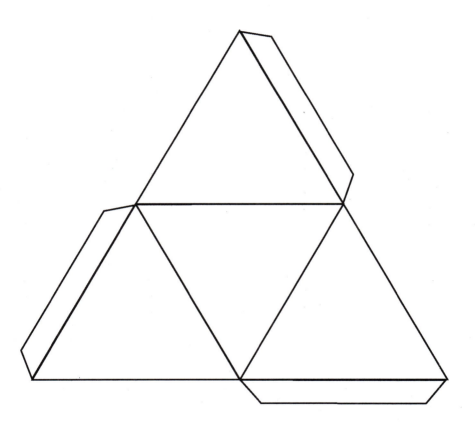

Big Idea 2

Minerals are the building blocks of all rocks. Every rock is made of at least one mineral, but more often two or more that have combined under conditions that allow for rock formation.

Dig It! • Lockwood DeWitt & B. K. Hixson

Dissecting Granite

Geologically Speaking ...

The very first concept we want you to grab onto is that minerals are the building blocks for rocks. Every single rock you pick up has at least one mineral, and most rocks contain two or more minerals. In honor of minerals' role as rock-builders, you are going to start examining an igneous rock and identifying the minerals in it.

Find a piece of granite or similar kind of rock. Granitoids—rocks similar to granite—are igneous rocks formed when large blobs of molten magma cool very slowly under the surface of the Earth. Because it cooled slowly, large crystals formed that can be seen with the naked eye.

Materials

1   Sample of a granite-like rock
1   Hand lens
1   Box of crayons
1   Pencil
1   Ruler
1   Pair of scissors
1   Piece of paper

Procedure

1. Using the hand lens, examine the rock sample under good light. Record the mineral colors that you see in the spaces below. If a mineral appears clear, write "colorless."

a._____

b._____

c._____

d._____

e._____

Dissecting Granite

2. The square below is exactly 1 inch by 1 inch. Cut an identical 1-inch square out of a piece of paper to make a window. Place the square window over your sample and, using your crayons and working in the box below, draw a picture of the minerals that you see.

3. Count the number of crystals of *mineral a* that you see inside the square. Then count the number of *mineral b, c, d,* and *e* crystals and record those numbers to the left of the / symbol. Divide each number by the total number of minerals visible to determine the percentage.

a._____ / _____ = _____%

b._____ / _____ = _____%

c._____ / _____ = _____%

d._____ / _____ = _____%

e._____ / _____ = _____%

4. Geologists use the percentage of each mineral present in a rock sample to classify the rock and assign it a name. Generally, these are technical names, but some geologists call their samples by names like "Brenda" or "Fred." (These geologists don't generally get published very often.)

5. Match the mineral descriptions in the following sentences to the minerals in your list in Step 3. Write the letter of the mineral that matches each description below.

_____ Hornblende is a black, shiny mineral.

_____ Quartz is generally colorless but may have a gray cast. Instead of breaking along flat planes like all the other minerals described here, quartz breaks like glass—every which way.

_____ Mica is very flat and shiny and is black to silvery-gray in appearance.

_____ You may have two varieties of feldspar; most often, one will be an off-white to light-gray color (plagioclase), and …

_____ The other is likely to have a light-pink to salmon color (alkali feldspar).

How Come, Huh?

The whole point of this lab is to underscore the idea that minerals are the building blocks for rocks. Another way of stating the obvious is to say that rocks are made of minerals.

Science Fair Extensions

6. Geologists use a process called "taking a thin section" to determine minerals' percentages more accurately than could be done using the technique that we showed you. Find out how this is done and why it is so much more accurate.

Ms. Stewart's Crystal Garden

Geologically Speaking ...

This next reaction produces crystals by evaporation. When the crystal-growing solution is poured onto the sponge, the sponge soaks up the liquid. The water in the sponge then slowly evaporates into the air. As it evaporates, it leaves behind the salts that were originally dissolved in the solution. What you have left are beautiful, and let us forewarn you, *extremely delicate* crystals.

Materials

- 50 mL table salt
- 10 mL ammonia
- 50 mL laundry bluing
- 100 mL water
- 1 Large bowl
- 1 Large spoon
- 1 Piece of sponge / rag / sock
- 1 Pie tin
- 1 Hand lens
- 1 Pair of goggles

The recipe that we are using to grow these crystals has been around for a long time. It incorporates salt, water, ammonia, and ferrous ferric hexacyanate, also known in washtub circles as laundry bluing, a whitener that is added to clothes.

One word of caution as you make your own crystal solution: *Avoid snorting fumes from the ammonia directly.*

Procedure

1. Obtain the first three materials from your local supermarket. Water can be obtained directly from the faucet. We don't care where you get the other items, but you will find them useful if you want to procede further.

2. Don your sporty OUPDs (Ocular Unit Protection Devices, also known as "goggles"), add everything to a large bowl, and stir. OK, not <u>everything</u> … just the first four materials from the list.

3. Place the sponge, rag, or sock in the pie tin and pour half the batch of crystal-growing solution over the sponge. Put the rest into a sealable jar or bottle for later use. Save it for a rainy day.

4. Place the pie tin in a warm location so that the solution will evaporate. The crystals will begin to appear in one to two hours and will continue to grow until all of the liquid has evaporated.

5. The sponge, rag, or sock will start to display a collection of very delicate, powdery crystals that will collapse if you touch or even breathe in their general direction. Definitely no sneezing. A hand lens will allow for close examination of these fine crystals.

If you have to move your crystals, also be forewarned that the slightest bump, bounce, or bonk will cause the crystals that you have created to collapse into a disappointing heap. If this happens, just add more solution and don't move them this time.

CRYSTAL SOLUTION

OLD SOCK

PIE TIN

Ms. Stewart's Crystal Garden

Data & Observations

Draw top-view pictures of your crystals at 1 hour, 3 hours, 24 hours, and 48 hours.

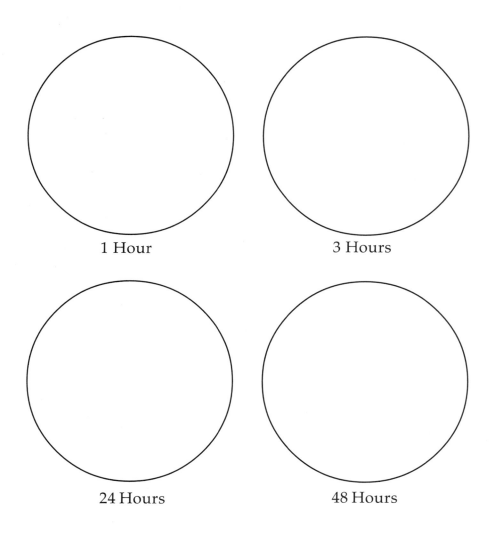

1 Hour

3 Hours

24 Hours

48 Hours

How Come, Huh?

In the previous lab, we looked at the fact that granitic rocks are made up of lots of minerals that you can see with the naked eye. In this lab, we are reversing the process. We added a whole bunch of chemicals together, poured them into a pan, and then let them evaporate to produce something new. The metaphors for this would be that the chemicals are minerals and the by-product is rock. It's a stretch, but the best we could do on short notice.

The main thing to take away from this section is that minerals are the building blocks for rocks. Rocks are made up of two or more minerals. Sometimes we can see the individual minerals with our naked eyes, but most of the time, we can't.

LIQUIDS EVAPORATE

SALTS REMAIN

CHEMICAL MIX

Science Fair Extensions

7. To add some color to your crystals, put drops of food coloring on the sponge / rag / sock right after you add the solution. As the solution is absorbed by the material, it migrates toward the surface of that object.

When it hits the food coloring, it absorbs it and carries it to the surface where it is redeposited with the other salts once the liquid evaporates.

8. This is strictly off the record, but these crystals will grow on any porous material. Try chunks of coal, charcoal briquettes, or pieces of soft wood like fir or pine.

Big Idea 3

Minerals can form from gases (sublimation), liquids (precipitation), and solids (recrystallization).

Caffeine Cathedrals

Geologically Speaking ...

You are going to use the process of sublimation to create crystals that can be seen with the naked eye. Sublimation is a term chemists give to chemicals and compounds that like to change directly from a solid to a gas without bothering to pass through the liquid phase. In this experiment, caffeine sublimates at about 178°C. The caffeine, once in a gas state, condenses on the bottom of the smaller, skinnier tube, forming small, white, needlelike crystals.

Materials

1   16 mm x 150 mm test tube
1   20 mm x 150 mm test tube
1   Votive candle
1   Book of matches
1   Hand lens
1   Wood splint
    Approx. 1/4 gram of caffeine powder
1   Pair of goggles

Procedure

1.   Put on your goggles. Grab the caffeine and dump it into the larger of the two test tubes.

2.   Slide the smaller test tube into the larger one so that the bottom of the small test tube is about 1 inch from the caffeine in the bottom of the larger test tube. Use the illustration shown here as a guide.

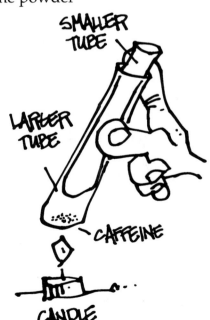

SMALLER TUBE

LARGER TUBE

CAFFEINE

CANDLE

Caffeine Cathedrals

3. With adult supervisior, light the candle. Hold the two test tubes over it. You will notice that some of the caffeine immediately starts to crystallize on the small test tube. As you continue to heat the two tubes, the remainder of the caffeine will sublimate into a gas.

4. After three or four min-utes, carefully remove the small test tube and look at the newly formed caffeine crystals on the bottom of it. This is where the hand lens comes in handy. Take the wood splint and pull out some of the long needles from inside the test tube. These are very fine crystals. The hand lens al-lows you to examine them more closely. Definitely a needlelike crys-tal habit, which we will get to in a minute.

5. Caffeine is a common ingredient in coffee, tea, and many soft drinks. So, when you wash the caffeine down the drain with a little bit of water, only the fish downstream will be affected.

Data & Observations

Draw a picture of the crystals that formed on the smaller of the two tubes.

How Come, Huh?

When the caffeine molecules get enough energy to turn to a vapor, they rise into the air above the liquid and cool very quickly— so quickly, in fact, that they do not have time to turn to a liquid again before becoming a solid. They lose the heat energy and immediately find their buddies that are forming crystals on the test tube. They join them.

Sublimation is pretty rare as a way to form crystals, but it does happen. One of the most common minerals to form this way is sulfur, around volcanic fumaroles. The only dormant volcano to ever have a mine near its summit in the United States was Mount Adams, in Southern Washington. The ore mined was sulfur (ores don't have to be metallic), and its mode of deposition was sublimation. There are other deposits of sulfur of this type that are still being mined today elsewhere in the world.

Another familiar mineral frequently formed by sublimation is one you might not initially think of as a mineral ... ice! Think back to our definition of a mineral: an inorganic, crystalline solid, with a distinct composition. Ice fits this definition, but because we generally don't think of it as a rock-forming material, we don't think of it as a mineral.

Science Fair Extensions

9. There are other compounds that sublimate. Dry ice, which is solid carbon dioxide, is one of the most notable compounds that does so. The solid transforms directly to a gas at room temperature. Check out our book, *Le Boom du Jour*, for ideas.

Test Tube Snowstorm

Geologically Speaking ...

Minerals and crystals form in a variety of ways. The next three experiments will allow you to observe crystal growth by evaporation, precipitation, and sublimation. We'd throw in hydrothermal deposits and igneous melts but the electric bill would suffer, so we are going to simply perform three relatively simple chemical reactions and let your imagination take over from there.

The first reaction produces crystals by precipitation. This word may conjure up images of rain or snow, but it also applies to crystal growth. Rain is produced when water droplets start to form on particles of dust in the air. As more and more molecules of water jump on the dust particle, the drop of water becomes heavier. When it finally gets too heavy for the cloud to hang onto, it drops to the ground.

In this experiment, two chemicals are mixed together. The alcohol causes the potassium sulfate molecules to start to clump together, forming crystals. When the crystals get too heavy to be supported by the liquid in the tube, they fall, or crash, to use chemists' terms, out of solution. It will be like having your own personal snowstorm, only you won't have to shovel the driveway.

Materials

1   16 mm x 150 mm test tube
1   Bottle of potassium sulfate solution (10%)
1   Bottle of isopropyl alcohol (70%)
1   1 mL pipette
1   Hand lens
1   Pair of goggles

Procedure

1. Affix protective eyewear firmly to the front of your face. Pour the 10% potassium sulfate solution into the test tube to fill the tube 2/3 to 3/4 of the way up. Cap the bottle to prevent any spills.

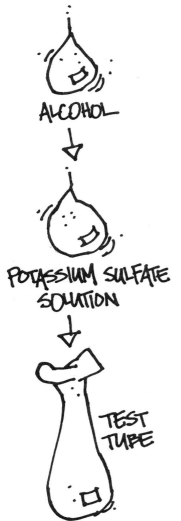

ALCOHOL

POTASSIUM SULFATE SOLUTION

TEST TUBE

2. Open the bottle of isopropyl alcohol, squeeze and fill the pipette, and slowly add 10 drops of alcohol to the test tube. You will immediately notice that a cloudy layer appears at the top of the tube. These are crystals starting to form.

3. Add a couple more drops of isopropyl alcohol to add to the snow-storm. At this point, take your hand lens and examine the crystals as they start to fall toward the bottom of the tube. The entire reaction takes about five minutes to complete, so hang in there.

4. You can pour everything down the drain when you are finished.

Data & Observations

On the lines below, describe what you saw.

_____

_____

_____

_____

_____

Test Tube Snowstorm

How Come, Huh?

Basically, the rubbing alcohol and the potassium sulfate do not like each other. When you add drops of rubbing alcohol to the solution, it causes the potassium sulfate to crash. In other words, the rubbing alcohol causes the molecules of potassium sulfate to clump together and form big crystals that we can see with the naked eye.

As these crystals get bigger and bigger, they start to weigh too much for the water in the solution to support them, so they fall very slowly to the bottom of the tube. As with weather, this is called precipitation. Another term for this is "crashing out of solution," and it is one of the ways that we can separate mixtures and solutions.

Science Fair Extensions

10. You were using a 10% solution to study the effect of isopropyl alcohol on that solution. Experiment with different concentrations to see if the size of the crystals is influenced.

11. Temperature creates all sorts of problems and solutions for chemists. Generally, the warmer a reaction is, the faster it takes place. Repeat this experiment, but try heating the potassium sulfate and then the isopropyl alcohol to see if the increased temperature makes a difference.

12. Try the experiment again, only cool the chemicals this time. Are the crystal sizes smaller? Do the crystals form at a slower rate?

Silica Crystal Garden

Geologically Speaking ...

You will add three different colored crystals to a glass jar containing water and a chemical called sodium silicate. As soon as the crystals enter the jar, they are surrounded by the silicate, which reacts with the metal in the crystal and forms a new compound that starts to grow toward the top of the liquid. When you are finished, the glass container will have gobs of long, skinny crystals growing from the bottom of the jar that look just like stalactites and stalagmites that can be found growing in limestone caves throughout the world. The crystals that are produced are all metal silicates. In order of appearance and color, they are copper (Cu) silicate, which is blue, nickel (Ni) silicate, which is green, and magnesium (Mg) silicate, which is white. Always respect any chemical that you work with and never touch or eat anything near it.

Materials

1   2 oz. bottle of sodium silicate
1   4 oz. glass jar with lid
1   Vial of mixed sulfate crystals:
      Copper sulfate crystals (sky blue)
      Nickel sulfate crystals (emerald green)
      Magnesium sulfate crystals (white)
1   Box of crayons or colored pencils

Procedure

1.   Open the bottle of sodium silicate and pour its contents into the glass jar. Fill the jar the rest of the way with water. Cap the jar and shake it vigorously to mix the two liquids together.

Silica Crystal Garden

2. Open the bottle of crystals and gently shake all of the chemical into the sodium silicate and water solution so that the crystals fall to the bottom. Immediately replace the lid on the jar and discard the bottle.

3. After the crystals have finished growing, they can be saved in the jar, or the liquid can be poured down the drain and the jar can be tossed into the garbage.

Data & Observations

Record the growth of the crystals in the spaces below and on the next page. If you have colored pencils available to you, use them to make a more accurate presentation.

SULFATE CRYSTALS

SODIUM SILICATE WATER MIX

10 minutes:_____	30 minutes:_____

```
┌─────────────────┐        ┌─────────────────┐
│                 │        │                 │
│                 │        │                 │
│                 │        │                 │
│                 │        │                 │
│                 │        │                 │
└─────────────────┘        └─────────────────┘
```

60 minutes:_____   90 minutes:_____

_____   _____

How Come, Huh?

There is a chemical reaction between the silicate in the solution and the metals in the salts. When they come in contact with one another, they combine to form a new chemical. These new atoms pile on top of one another in solution. This creates the long, skinny crystals that you see in your jar.

Science Fair Extensions

13. There is another very interesting reaction that occurs with sodium silicate and rubbing alcohol. Pour equal amounts of the two liquids into a jar, stir, and they form a polymer-like sphere.

14. Magnesium sulfate can be mixed into solution and added to two cups. This will cause a yarn that connects the cups to grow stalactites and stalagmites.

SILICATE ION

SULFATE CRYSTAL

Pickled Jewelry

Geologically Speaking ...

Crystals can also be formed when they recrystallize from a solution onto a substrate (anchor). If the process is allowed to take place slowly enough, large, beautiful crystals can form. In the case of this lab, you are going to dissolve a common household pickling spice, alum, into solution. When you seed a pipe cleaner with crystals and insert it into the solution, the result will be a beautiful, crystal bracelet that will be the envy of your friends.

Materials

ALUM

WATER

500 ML BEAKER

1   Bottle of alum
    (Aluminum potassium sulfate)
1   Craft stick
1   Beaker, 500 mL
    Water, warm
1   12 oz. cup
1   8 inch length of string
1   Pencil
1   Pipe cleaner

Procedure

1. Fill the beaker with 400 mL of warm or hot water.

2. Add a sprinkle of alum to the beaker and stir with the craft stick. If all of the crystals dissolve, which they should at first, add more. Keep adding and stirring until it becomes harder and harder to dissolve the crystals.

3. When you get to the point where no more crystals will dissolve, you have a saturated solution.

4. Bend the pipe cleaner into a circle and twist the ends together.

5. Tie the string to the side of the pipe cleaner and then slide the string onto the pencil. Use the illustration at the right as a guide. Hang the pipe cleaner inside the cup.

6. Pour the saturated solution of alum into the cup and over the pipe cleaner. Set the cup in an area where it can stand undisturbed for several days.

How Come, Huh?

The pipe cleaner acted as a substrate, or anchor, for the dissolved alum particles floating around in the solution. They tend to not like to do that; if they can find a place to park and grow, they will do that, instead. Once a crystal starts to grow, others will join in. Over time, you get a beautiful set of crystals.

Science Fair Extensions

15. Try the same experiment, but use a super saturated solution of sugar.

Popcorn Rock Crystals

Geologically Speaking ...

The piece of dolomite that is in your possession is actually somewhat unique and possesses an interesting property that is not necessarily common to other dolomites: It grows aragonite crystals when it is placed in distilled, white vinegar. This characteristic was first discovered in 1981 by Richard D. Barnes.

Typically, horn corals are preserved in limestone, a rock that is composed of calcium carbonate, which reacts with vinegar and dissolves in that weak acid so that the fossil can be recovered and studied. The interesting thing about this rock is that it did not dissolve but, rather, produced spectacular, white, bulbous crystals, resembling popped kernels of corn. That is how the rock got its commercial name, popcorn rock.

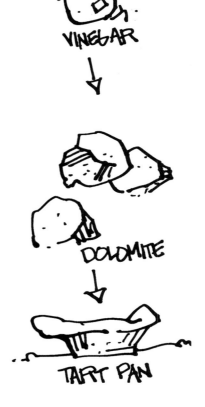

VINEGAR

DOLOMITE

TART PAN

Materials

3   Samples of dolomite
1   Tart pan, 5-inch diameter
1   16 oz. bottle of vinegar

Procedure

1. Place the dolomite in the tart pan and add the vinegar. The rock should be two-thirds covered.

2. Place the tart pan in a warm, sunny location, so that the solution will evaporate. The crystals will begin to appear in one to two hours and continue to grow until all of the liquid has evaporated.

3. Once the crystals have formed on the top surface of the dolomite, gently pick the specimen up and examine the underside. You may find fine, needle-like crystals that were produced on the underside of the rock. Keep in mind that not all rocks have the same chemical composition and that other conditions may affect the growth of the crystals.

Data & Observations

Record the growth of the crystals in the spaces below.

Day 1 Notes:_____
_____

Day 2 Notes:_____
_____

Day 3 Notes:_____
_____

Day 4 Notes:_____
_____

Popcorn Rock Crystals

How Come, Huh?

All rocks are porous and can and will absorb liquids. In this case, the dolomite absorbs the vinegar. The vinegar, like all liquids, migrates toward the top of the rocks. Along the way, it dissolves part of the rock and takes it with it. Dolomite, being rich in magnesium, contributes the chemicals to the effort.

When the vinegar and dissolved magnesium get to the surface of the rock, the liquid evaporates, leaving behind a mineral called aragonite. This mineral can form as a bulbous blob of hard, white stuff, which resembles popcorn kernels.

Science Fair Extensions

16. With the supervision of an adult, you can make your own acetic acid using glacial acidic acid. Mix and pour different concentrations of the acid into a pan with the dolomite and observe the effects that it has on the rock.

17. Compare the effect of acetic acid (vinegar) on dolomite with the same chemical immersed in limestone and then, also, the mineral calcite. Do a little research to find out what happened in both cases that is different from what happened with the dolomite.

Big Idea 4

Each mineral has a unique set of properties and can be identified using a series of standardized tests.

A Word About

Mineral identification can be frustrating, especially at the beginning. The skills involved require practice and experience; this means it can be difficult at first. But with time, it will begin to feel natural to heft a sample as you pick it up, to judge its specific gravity. At a glance, you will notice the cleavage planes and their quality. At the same time, you might recognize familiar shapes that give you an important clue as to what the mineral is. You will automatically register the sample's luster and color. And you will have all these things in your head within a couple of seconds after you lean over to grab it.

Another thing to be aware of as you start is that there are about 2,000 different recognized minerals. That seems like an overwhelming number to deal with, but actually, there are fewer than 100 that are common enough to worry about. Of those, about a dozen minerals or mineral families make up the vast bulk of rocks. Learning just these is a fantastic start. Others are so distinctive and interesting that they're easy to learn. In this section, we provide mineral profiles on 8 different minerals and mineral families. Some are common and abundant, like quartz and calcite, and make up a great deal of the Earth we see.

Mineral ID

In this book, the word "common" should be taken to mean widely distributed—that is, something you might find anywhere—while "abundant" means that it occurs in large quantity. So quartz and calcite are common and abundant, while pyrite and magnetite are both common, but not abundant in most places. Some minerals, like talc, are very abundant in certain areas but are restricted to those areas and are not seen elsewhere.

There are tests to determine properties that are most useful in identifying a particular mineral. Determining a mineral's "occurence" is important because certain minerals tend to occur in certain geological environments. Recognize the environment, and you have a good clue as to what minerals you might or might not find.

Finally, it is important to understand that, with few exceptions, it is impossible to identify a mineral on the basis of a single property. The gold color and metallic luster of a mineral might suggest pyrite, but you have to check the streak to make sure it's not actually gold.

Mineral Selection

You can perform the 8 tests on the next pages with any mineral that you like. However, we have compiled a list of 8 minerals that will give you a good, basic introduction to the tests and allow you to see definite results. All of these minerals are available to you from most rock shops, as well as from the vendors listed in the front of this book, including us, of course.

The List

___ Amethyst   ___ Azurite
___ Calcite   ___ Lodestone
___ Mica   ___ Rose Quartz
___ Talc   ___ Pyrite

Before We Get Going ...

Geologically Speaking ...

Just as the letters of the alphabet combine to make words, the elements of the periodic table combine to make any compound known to man. Minerals are the building blocks that combine to make up all of the rocks found on Earth. Minerals combine in different forms and quantities to make the rocks that you see in landforms.

Every mineral has a different set of unique characteristics, and there are several tests that are used to separate and identify common minerals. These tests are color, hardness, streak, crystal shape, specific gravity, and optical properties tests, to name a few. There are over 2,000 different kinds of minerals that have been discovered and identified. Each mineral is unique and produces its own individual set of characteristics. Some (diamonds) are very hard and others (gypsum or talc) are very soft. They come in every color and almost every shape you can imagine. The purpose of this lab is to acquaint you with these tests and give you a taste of mineral identification.

A brief description of each test is outlined below. At first blush it may seem to be a bit overwhelming, but after you work through each of the tests and have time to digest the information, you will find that the task of identifying minerals is not so daunting.

Mineral Tests

1. *Color Test:* Look at the color of the mineral and record what you see. This test is accurate for monochromatic (single color) minerals but is deceiving for multicolored minerals.

2. *Streak Test:* Scratch the mineral across the surface of a ceramic tile (herein known as a streak plate). The mineral produces a color that is either similar to the visible color of the mineral or different. This is one of the definitive tests you will learn and is used extensively in mineral keys.

3. *Luster Test:* The surface of the mineral is described using 1 of 6 common terms.

4. *Mohs' Hardness Test*: This determines how hard the mineral is, compared to a standard set of minerals. You will take each one of your mineral samples and attempt to scratch it with your fingernail, a copper penny, a steel nail, and a piece of glass. Depending on the results that you find, you can determine the relative hardness of the mineral.

5. *Specific Gravity Test:* Another word to describe this test would be density. The arrangement of the atoms inside the minerals determines how densely the mineral is packed. Therefore, the density can be determined by dividing the mass of the mineral by its volume.

6. *Cleavage & Fracture Test:* This describes how easily the mineral splits. It may split along a single edge or along as many as 6 edges. Examine each mineral you have and try to determine how many "clean" edges can be produced by splitting it.

7. *Magnetism Test:* Some iron-bearing minerals have a magnetic field that surrounds them. If a mineral attracts and collects iron filings, it tests positive for magnetism.

8. *Fizz Test:* This is also called the acid test. Vinegar is a dilute acid. When it is placed on the surface of some minerals, it reacts chemically to produce gas, which creates fizzing. This test specifically identifies minerals in the carbonate group.

Mineral Color

Geologically Speaking ...

The color of a mineral is directly influenced by the chemicals it contains. If the mineral is monochromatic, meaning one (mono) color (chromatic), this is a very reliable test. If the mineral is multicolored, meaning many colors, then you will have to rely on other tests to name the sample in question.

For example, azurite is a monochromatic mineral. It always looks blue, no matter where you find it. However, quartz is a multicolored mineral that can be found around the world as any of the following: quartz crystals (colorless), amethyst (purple), rose quartz (pink), smoky quartz (gray), milky quartz (white), and citrine (yellow).

Materials

8   Mineral samples (amethyst, azurite, calcite, lodestone, mica, rose quartz, talc, pyrite)

1   Hand lens

Procedure

1. All 8 of the mineral samples should have a distinctly different color.

2. Examine all 8 minerals in the order listed in the data table on the next page. Enter the color or colors that you see in the space next to the name of the mineral.

Data & Observations

Below, provide color descriptions of the mineral samples. Note additional colors, changes in color, or any impurities and imperfections that you may find in each sample.

Sample	Color(s) of Specimen
Amethyst	_____
Azurite	_____
Calcite	_____
Lodestone	_____
Mica	_____
Rose Quartz	_____
Talc	_____
Pyrite	_____

How Come, Huh?

Among geologists, color is often spoken of as a "dangerous" property because it can be very misleading. Students just getting started tend to rely more on color than is wise; other characteristics take some practice and familiarity before their usefulness becomes clear. Still, color is a property that people are used to observing. It will always be one of the easiest to observe, and it's sometimes useful.

Calcite is a mineral that varies tremendously in color. Some minerals come in variable colors, but the range of variation is fairly small. Pyrite can range from a very light gold that almost looks silver to a brassy or coppery color, but it's accurate to say that it tends toward gold.

Mineral Color

As a general rule, minerals that are colorless or white in their absolutely pure form are easily colored by small amounts of impurities. A tiny amount of iron, just a fraction of a percent, can color a mineral red, orange, yellow, or earthy-green, depending on how much oxygen is present. So when you're using a mineral identification key and one of the colors for a mineral is noted as white or colorless, you can anticipate that the mineral may vary a great deal.

Because artificial light often has its own distinct color, the best place to make color observations is under sunlight. Often you can see a noticeable difference within a single room, depending on whether you examine the mineral by the window or under a lightbulb. Overall, no single property alone should be used to identify minerals. The best way to deal with color is practice. Sometimes you can trust it; sometimes you can't. Experience helps.

Mineral Profile: Quartz

Quartz is one of the most common (occuring in many different places), abundant (occuring in large quantities), and chemically simple minerals. Also, of common minerals, it's one of the hardest (7 on the Mohs' scale—more about this later). Because it is so abundant, it tends to be one of the most familiar mineral names; people tend to call any shiny, colorless mineral quartz. Frequently they're wrong, but it's not a bad first guess.

Quartz occurs as a major component of many different kinds of rocks. For example, granite ranges from 10 to 25 percent quartz by volume. Sandstone and quartzite (metamorphosed sandstone) get near 100 percent quartz. But most people think of quartz as the beautiful crystals, often vividly colored, that fill pockets and holes in rock. These kinds of crystals form when water dissolves quartz from one place and then redeposits it in a hole. Some of the largest and nicest of these crystals are formed as the result of hot water action, but hot water isn't necessary.

Quartz is also the mineral that makes up the stones rock-hounds look for: agates and jasper. Both of these are actually made of quartz, but the crystals are so tiny, you can't see them without a microscope. Sometimes, you can't even see them then. Agate is banded and translucent, while jasper is unbanded and nearly opaque.

Science Fair Extensions

18. Collect the whole family of quartz: crystals (colorless), amethyst (purple), rose quartz (pink), smoky quartz (gray), milky quartz (white), and citrine (yellow). Do some reading and determine what it is that gives each type of quartz its particular color.

Streak Test

Geologically Speaking ...

This is one of the two most valuable mineral identification tests, the other being the hardness test that is coming up in a couple of pages. The streak test can help you determine if a mineral is monochromatic (a single color) or multicolored (a combination of colors). Most mineral identification guides use the streak color to separate and identify minerals.

Materials

8   Mineral samples (amethyst, azurite, calcite, lodestone, mica, rose quartz, talc, pyrite)
1   Streak plate
1   Pencil

Procedure

1. Before you start, return to the previous lab and enter the color of each mineral specimen into the data table on the next page.

2. Pick a mineral up with your writing hand. Hold the streak plate firmly, with the thumb and index finger of your other hand on the table. Beginning at the top edge of the streak plate, draw a straight line down to the other edge of the streak plate with the mineral.

3. Examine the color of the streak, and record your observations in the data table on the next page. The streak color is actually the color of the powdered mineral, which may be different from the color of the whole crystal.

4. Test all your minerals in order. You do not need to clean the streak plate between tests. Simply make the streak on different parts of the plate. If your streak plate starts to get grubby and you want to clean it, scouring powder and an old toothbrush do a good job.

Data & Observations

Sample	Color of Specimen	Streak
Amethyst	_____	_____
Azurite	_____	_____
Calcite	_____	_____
Lodestone	_____	_____
Mica	_____	_____
Rose Quartz	_____	_____
Talc	_____	_____
Pyrite	_____	_____

How Come, Huh?

If you have read the section on color, you know that some minerals vary greatly in that property. The nice thing about the streak test is that a single kind of mineral will always have the same streak color. When you rub a mineral on a rough surface that's harder than the mineral itself, the mineral is ground away a bit, leaving a powdered sample on the rough surface. The color of that powder is the streak. The standard surface that's used is an unglazed porcelain tile—rough, hard, and white, so that the color shows well. However, some minerals are harder (quartz and others), and if you try to get a streak from those, you'll just scratch the streak plate.

Streak Test

The streak test's usefulness is clear in the case of hematite. Hematite comes in two major forms which look completely different. Specular hematite is silvery-gray and metallic, while earthy hematite is reddish-brown and dull. But in both cases, the streak is an earthy-red. Another good example is pyrite, or fool's gold. Pyrite gives an almost black streak, which may look a little greenish-brown. Real gold will give a golden streak. Be forewarned: If you test this with your mother's jewelry, you will be a long streak on the floor.

The upshot is this: The streak test can be very useful for certain minerals, but not all. As with conducting all the other tests here, practice and familiarity are important.

Mineral Profile: Pyrite

Pyrite is commonly referred to by the name "fool's gold" because its color and luster are similar to those of gold. Whether or not a would-be miner has ever really mistaken it for gold, we can't say, but it would be a good story. Among minerals with a metallic luster, pyrite is probably the most common of all. It can show up as a trace mineral (less than 2 percent) in most rocks, particularly intrusive igneous, dark-colored, meta-morphic and organic-rich (also dark-colored) sedimentary rocks. It is most abundant in ore deposits, where it is generally considered a nuisance. It is not currently feasible to smelt iron from pyrite, but particularly nice samples are sold as collectible specimens.

Pyrite forms in oxygen-poor environments. When there's plenty of organic material (read this as dead stuff) buried away from air, carbon will grab all the oxygen it can get, leaving iron stuck with sulfur. So fossils are sometimes crusted with a beautiful sprinkling of pyrite, and the "pyrite sand dollars" you sometimes see for sale form as flattened plates under beds of coal. They're not really fossils at all, but they're still spectacular. When pyrite is exposed to air and moisture long enough, the iron will start to grab oxygen and water and turn into rust.

Science Fair Extensions

19. Collect and display monochromatic and multicolored minerals next to their streak plates. Further separate the minerals into groups that have the same streak color as their appearance and those that present a different color for their streak pattern. Look at the chemical composition of each mineral for clues as to why they appear in the group that they do.

20. Minerals are crushed and used as pigments to color paint, metals, and other items. Find out which minerals are used as pigments and how the process works. Once you know a particular mineral is used as a coloring pigment, crush it, add it to white paint, and demonstrate how the coloring process works.

21. Figure out a way that you could see the streak of the harder minerals, like quartz, when they simply scratch the tile that other minerals streak.

Luster

Geologically Speaking ...

Luster describes the way light is reflected off the surface of a mineral. The type and intensity of the luster varies from mineral to mineral, depending on the characteristics of the mineral's surface and the amount of light that is absorbed.

Common terms are used to describe the luster of minerals and, as a general rule, do not need much explanation. We have substituted the word *glassy* for vitreous. Other than that, *dull, pearly, silky, greasy,* and *metallic,* six of the seven dwarves, should be easy to apply to the light reflected off the mineral to your eyes.

Materials

8   Mineral samples (amethyst, azurite, calcite, lodestone, mica, rose quartz, talc, pyrite)
1   Bright light (sunlight is best)
1   Hand lens

Procedure

1. Examine the first mineral under a bright light or in direct sunlight to evaluate its luster. If you are having a difficult time deciding between two descriptions, it is entirely acceptable to mark two. For example, a mineral can have both a dull and a metallic luster.

2. Describe the luster of your samples. Make note if the luster of a mineral varies from place to place. Use the terms *glassy, dull, metallic, silky, greasy,* and *pearly.*

Data & Observations

Sample	Luster	Streak
Amethyst	_____	_____
Azurite	_____	_____
Calcite	_____	_____
Lodestone	_____	_____
Mica	_____	_____
Rose Quartz	_____	_____
Talc	_____	_____
Pyrite	_____	_____

How Come, Huh?

Luster describes the way light is reflected off the surface of a mineral. The type and intensity of the luster varies from mineral to mineral, depending on the characteristics of the mineral's surface and the amount of light that is absorbed.

Determining the way light is reflected off a mineral to your eyes is important in terms of being able to identify the mineral.

Luster

Luster is a mineral property that is strongly affected by weathering. As a mineral spends more and more time exposed to air and moisture, the chemical components of the mineral slowly combine with water, oxygen, or other substances to form new compounds. The new compounds are commonly tiny flecks of minerals like clay or rust—both of which are pretty dull. So a mineral that is glassy on a freshly broken surface may be dull on a weathered surface. It's often helpful to have both kinds of surfaces on a rock sample. In granite, for example, the quartz doesn't weather, but stays glassy looking. Feldspar does weather; on a fresh surface, it will look glassy on cleavage planes, but on a weathered surface, it will look progressively duller and duller as weathering takes place.

Luster can also vary from one place to another on the same mineral. Micas are glassy on cleavage planes but dull at the edges. Feldspar is glassy on its good cleavages but waxy-to-dull on fractured surfaces.

Mineral Profile: Talc

Talc is the softest of minerals, number 1 on Mohs' hardness scale. Rock made almost entirely of talc is called "soapstone," due to its soapy, greasy feel. Because of its softness, soapstone is easy to shape, and sculptors of many times and cultures have created beautiful works of art from this rock. It is also very inactive chemically, so it was once widely used for tabletops in laboratories. Its most important use now is in powdered form, as a carrier for various substances. As a powder, it helps things disperse evenly rather than in clumps. We have probably all used talcum baby powder at one time or another (even if we don't remember it), but talc is also used in paints, insecticides, rubber, paper, ceramics, and other products.

To form, talc requires a rather narrow set of conditions. First, rocks very high in magnesium are required. These frequently are derived from the Earth's mantle, which is a big requirement right off the bat. Then, with a little water around, these rocks must be exposed to relatively low temperature and pressure, and talc will form.

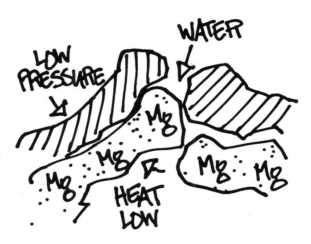

Because of these requirements, talc is not as widespread as many other minerals, and is found near prehistoric plate edges, where mantle rocks have been brought up and mixed into rocks that end up at the surface.

Science Fair Extensions

22. Talc is used in many, many commercial applications. For starters, it is used in talcum powder, an absorbent powder that is used to help keep babies dry. It is also used as the base in a number of cosmetic products, as an additive/filler in medications, and as a dessicant in air filters. Do some research and find out at least 10 more everyday products that use talc.

23. Compare the luster readings for minerals with those used for pearls. Talk with a gemologist and find out how pearls are graded, and why they are different colors, shapes, and lusters. Compare and contrast pearls with minerals.

Mohs' Hardness Test

Geologically Speaking ...

This is another valuable test to help determine the name of a mineral. The hardness of a mineral is determined by the strength of the bonds holding the atoms together inside the mineral. To determine the hardness of your mineral samples, you will use a scale that was first devised in 1812 by Friedrich Mohs and is still used today. Mohs selected 10 common minerals for his scale and arranged them in order from softest to hardest.

You will test each mineral by scratching it on four common items. The relative hardness of these items is listed in parentheses: your fingernail (2.5), a copper penny (3), a steel nail (5.5), and quartz (7).

Materials

8   Mineral samples (amethyst, azurite, calcite, lodestone, mica, rose quartz, talc, pyrite)
1   Copper penny
1   Fingernail (yours)
1   Steel nail
1   Sample of quartz

Procedure

1. Scratch mineral sample #1 with your fingernail. If it produces a scratch, put an x in the *Finger* column. If it does not produce a scratch, leave it blank. Test all of the minerals with your fingernail. Then test each mineral using the three other items.

2. The "Hardness Rule" is pretty simple: A substance will scratch anything that is as hard as it is, or softer. It will be scratched by anything that is the same hardness or harder. Sometimes you need to be careful because a soft mineral might leave a powder trail (see Streak Test), which may look like a scratch but really isn't. Because the hardness rule applies to anything, we can use everyday objects as well as standard minerals. As your knowledge and collection of samples grows, you can use samples to narrow the hardness down even moreso than we will do here.

3. To determine the relative hardness of each mineral, choose the last item that it scratched and select the next number on the column as the relative hardness. For example, if mineral #1 scratched your fingernail and the penny but not the steel nail, you would list the relative hardness as 4. If a mineral scratches all of the items, list it as 8+. If it scratches none of the items, list it as 1. If a sample both scratches and is scratched by another sample, the two samples have the same hardness. That doesn't prove they're the same thing.

Data & Observations

Sample Name	Finger(2.5)	Copper(3)	Steel(5.5)	Quartz(7)
1._____	_____	_____	_____	_____
2._____	_____	_____	_____	_____
3._____	_____	_____	_____	_____
4._____	_____	_____	_____	_____
5._____	_____	_____	_____	_____
6._____	_____	_____	_____	_____
7._____	_____	_____	_____	_____
8._____	_____	_____	_____	_____

Mohs' Hardness Test

How Come, Huh?

As you have learned, Mohs hardness test is another valuable test to help determine the identity of a mineral. The hardness of a mineral is determined by the strength of the bonds holding the atoms together inside the mineral. To determine the hardness of your mineral samples, you will conduct Mohs' hardness test. As you now know, Friedrich Mohs selected 10 common minerals for his scale and arranged them in order from softest to hardest. The complete list of minerals on Mohs' scale is shown below. Minerals harder than quartz are not encountered frequently, and are uncommon enough that many of them are gemstones.

1. Talc
2. Gypsum
3. Calcite
4. Fluorite
5. Apatite
6. Feldspar
7. Quartz
8. Topaz
9. Corundum
10. Diamond

Dig It! • Lockwood LeWitt & B. K. Hixson

Mineral Profile: Feldspar

Unlike most of the other examples in our famous mineral profiles, "feldspar" is not a single mineral, but rather, it is the name of a group, or family, of minerals. Like most families, this one has certain characteristics that make it distinct. First, the minerals' compositions are similar, with variation in the amounts of the elements, calcium, sodium, and potassium. The calcium- and sodium-rich group is called plagioclase feldspar, while the potassium- and sodium-rich group group is called alkali feldspar. Second, their crystal structures and physical properties are similar, so without practice, it can be very difficult to tell one from another. Third, their kinds of occurrence are similar: very common and very abundant.

Because of their abundance, the feldspars are an important group to know, but because of their similarities, they are one of the more difficult to learn. Most igneous and metamorphic rocks will have one or two kinds of feldspars as major components. Look for cleavage to distinguish these from quartz—quartz has no cleavage. Feldspars also weather to clay. In fact, most clay in soils comes from weathered feldspars. Quartz tends to be transparent and doesn't weather at all, while feldspars tend to be translucent or opaque to the naked eye and get cloudy with weathering.

The single characteristic that you can use to distinguish plagioclase from alkali feldspars is that plagioclase usually has a feature called twinning. A single crystal is actually made up of numerous parallel sets of planes that are related to one another. When you see light reflecting off a cleavage face, you may see parallel bright and dark lines, called *striations*. Turn the crystal a little bit, and the dark lines will turn bright and the bright lines will go dark. Alkali feldspar does not show striations.

Science Fair Extensions

24. Explain why using Mohs' hardness test on rocks is not an appropriate use of this test.

Specific Gravity

Geologically Speaking ...

For our purposes, the specific gravity of a mineral is synonymous with the density. The density of an object can be determined by weighing the object (in grams) and dividing it by its volume (in cubic centimeters). For example, water has a density of 1, meaning that 1 gram of water occupies 1 cubic centimeter of space. Most minerals have a density of between 2 and 3. The place where specific gravity is going to be useful to you as a budding geologist is in recognizing samples that seem extraordinarily light or extraordinarily heavy <u>for their size</u>.

Materials

8   Mineral samples (amethyst, azurite, calcite, lodestone, mica, rose quartz, talc, pyrite)
1   Piece of pumice
1   Piece of obsidian
1   Lead fishing weight
1   Styrofoam cup
2   Hands (yours)

Procedure

1. Find two rock samples that are as close to each other in size as possible; hold one in each hand. Bounce them a little bit (drop your hands so the samples are suspended for a moment but never really leave your hands). Now switch the samples between hands. Can you feel a difference in heft?

2. If you have two samples of the same kind of rock/mineral, but they are of different sizes, repeat the procedure in Step 1 with these two. Because they're the same kind of rock, they have the same specific gravity (which means they have the same density and heft). You should notice a distinct difference in weight, but your eyes and your fingers are telling you that the size is different, too. Your mind and your body together learn to distinguish heft.

3. If you have a metallic mineral like pyrite or galena, try hefting it. Can you tell that this sample feels "too heavy" for its size? If you have a piece of pumice, can you tell that it feels "too light"?

4. Try this out with a lead fishing weight and a piece of styrofoam. If you haven't quite gotten the idea yet, this will make it clear. Lead is really heavy for its size; styrofoam is really light for its size.

5. Go through your samples and repeat the procedure in Step 1. Try ranking the samples in terms of heft. We're sorry that we can't provide an answer key for this. However, mineral reference books do provide density. The property may be noted as either specific gravity or density. Just remember, the number means how many times the density of water. "Normal" for rocks is about 2 to 3, and rocks and minerals outside this range just don't feel quite right.

Specific Gravity

Data & Observations

Compare all of your specimens with one another and rank them from least specific gravity (lightest) to most.

Sample	Color	Heft
Amethyst	_____	_____
Azurite	_____	_____
Calcite	_____	_____
Lodestone	_____	_____
Mica	_____	_____
Rose Quartz	_____	_____
Talc	_____	_____
Pyrite	_____	_____

How Come, Huh?

What we mean here is that a chunk of quartz the size of a car is gonna be heavy; a chunk too small to see is gonna be light. Simple. But some materials feel way too heavy or way too light for a normal hand-sized piece. These are the ones that should get your attention.

For example, minerals with a metallic luster (see the Luster test in this section, if that word sounds Greek to you) will tend to have high specific gravities. Barite is a startling mineral;

it's normally light-colored, and at a glance looks like a quartz/feldspar type rock, like sandstone, granite, or gneiss. But you pick it up, and it feels twice as heavy as it ought to. That should get your attention and tell you that you have something odd.

At the other end of the spectrum, we have things like pumice, which is so light, it's silly. Geology students through the ages have had pictures taken with 4-foot boulders of pumice in their arms. Pumice will float on water, it's so light (for its size).

And the truth is, this is exactly the way professional geologists use this property. They call it "heft," and like most of the other tests discussed here, it's a matter of judgment, familiarity, and practice. They pick up a sample, maybe toss it in the air and catch it, toss it from one hand to another, or with pebble-sized pieces, rattle them around in a cupped hand. They often look like they're doing this absentmindedly, not paying a whole lot of attention to what they're doing. But in the back of their minds, what they're thinking is, "How does this compare to the hefts of all the other rocks I've handled?" Professional geologists only rarely try to get a precise measurement of density or specific gravity.

Specific Gravity

Mineral Profile: Galena

Galena is a distinctive and often beautiful mineral. With its metallic luster, cubic form, and extraordinary heft (specific gravity), it is difficult to mistake for anything else.

Galena is nearly the only significant source of lead. It is found commonly in ore deposits, not only of lead, but as an accessory in deposits of other metals. Interestingly, silver can substitute for lead in the crystal structure, and most samples of galena have some silver in them. I don't want to mislead you: The silver is chemically combined, and not really extractable except in laboratory or industrial settings. You're not going to break open a chunk of galena and find a nugget of silver inside it. When the galena is mined and smelted for its lead content, this silver can be recovered, and add some real dollars to the value of the lead. In mining operations, this kind of extra goodie is called "frosting" (really)!

One of the largest deposits of galena in the U.S. is in the tristate area of Missouri, Oklahoma, and Kansas. These deposits are associated with the ore of zinc, sphalerite. They are also poor in silver, compared to many other deposits. Other important deposits are found in Idaho, Colorado, and Utah. Leadville, Colorado got its name from the galena deposits there, which are also quite rich in silver.

Science Fair Extensions

25. Locate a triple beam balance and a graduated cylinder. Check out the formula for density listed below:

$$\text{Density} = \text{mass}/\text{volume} \ (\text{or}) \ d = m/v$$

Weigh your mineral specimens, determine the volume by plunking them into the graduated cylinder, and calculate the density of each mineral specimen. When you are done with the actual calculating, compare your hand-weighed results with the actual measurements that were taken using scales and balances.

Cleavage & Fracture

Geologically Speaking ...

Cleavage and fracture are actually two properties that can be tested simultaneously. The first one, cleavage, describes the shapes that are produced when a mineral is whacked with a hammer and broken into smaller pieces. This is obviously not going to be a good idea, because you probably have only one sample of each mineral, and bashing your collection to bits hardly sounds like a good idea to anyone that we have met. So, suffice it to say, we are simply going to describe this test for you.

Once the mineral specimen has been broken, the geologist examines the sample for smooth surfaces. These may be cubes, rhombohedrons, or simply very flat surfaces (planes). When describing the fracture and cleavage of a mineral, data tables always include *cleavage* first and *fracture* afterward.

Fracture can be described as the surfaces of separation other than the cleaved planes, or the faces that are left over. The terms that are used to describe the fracture are *conchoidal* (shell-like), *uneven*, *hackly* (like the hairs on the back of a dog that is mad), and *jagged*.

Materials

8 Mineral samples
    Amethyst
    Azurite
    Calcite
    Lodestone
    Mica
    Rose quartz
    Talc
    Pyrite
1 Hand lens
    Good light (sunlight is best)

Cleavage & Fracture

Procedure

Examine each of your samples carefully with the hand lens. Try to catch little sparkles from flat surfaces; these will be cleavages. If you can find cleavage, describe it as *perfect, good,* or *poor* in the data table. If you can't, write *none* in the cleavage column. Remember, there may be more than one description that fits. In the fracture section, describe broken surfaces that are not flat planes; the terms to be checked off here are *shell-like, uneven, hackly,* and *jagged.* Some minerals, like calcite and galena, rarely if ever show fracture, so write *none* for samples that show cleavages on all surfaces.

Data & Observations

Examine each of the minerals you have, and do your best to identify the fracture of each sample. If you are uncertain, leave that row blank. It is better to omit information than provide misinformation.

Sample	Color	Cleavage	Fracture Shell-like	Uneven	Hackly	Jagged
1	Purple	_____	_____	_____	_____	_____
2	Blue	_____	_____	_____	_____	_____
3	White	_____	_____	_____	_____	_____
4	Gray	_____	_____	_____	_____	_____
5	Silver	_____	_____	_____	_____	_____
6	Pink	_____	_____	_____	_____	_____
7	Green	_____	_____	_____	_____	_____
8	Gold	_____	_____	_____	_____	_____

How Come, Huh?

Cleavage and fracture are simply ways of describing how a mineral breaks. Breaking rocks is a lot of fun; every time you do it, you have an opportunity to see something that no one has ever seen before.

The first property, cleavage, indicates that a mineral breaks along certain very flat surfaces, or planes. The quality of a cleavage plane is related to its cleanness. Glass-smooth breaks are called *perfect*. These can be recognized on a fresh break because they reflect light like little mirrors or panes of glass. Less clean breaks may look a little dull but may still sparkle in good light. These are called *good* cleavages. *Poor* cleavages will produce planes that are clearly flat, but that are dull and generally ragged. A mineral may have more than one cleavage plane, and these different cleavages may have different qualities. For example, the feldspar has two cleavages: one perfect (glassy), and one poor/good (pretty dull, but pretty distinct). These two planes cross at about right angles. This is a good way to recognize feldspar and distinguish it from quartz, which has no cleavage. If a mineral doesn't have cleavage planes, then the broken surfaces are called fractures.

Fractures can be described as the surfaces of separation other than the cleaved planes, or the faces that are left over. The terms that are used to describe fractures are *conchoidal* (shell-like), *uneven*, *hackly* (like the hairs on the back of a dog that is mad), and *jagged*. A mineral may have more than one cleavage AND have a distinct fracture. Going back to feldspar, the ends of the blocks formed by the two cleavages show an uneven fracture. Quartz and pyrite both show conchoidal fractures.

Cleavage & Fracture

A bit more on cleavage: A set of parallel planes is considered ONE cleavage. Imagine a fresh ream of paper; each sheet is parallel to and identical to every other sheet. You could split the ream anywhere, and that split would be just like any other split. So you can split a chunk of mica into thinner sheets just about forever, but all the different splits are one cleavage because they're all parallel. The same applies to minerals that have notable symmetry.

Imagine a neat stack of tiny, little cubes, let's say arranged into a giant cube that is 1,000 tiny cubes on each side. You would not be able to tell one side from another. Each of the six faces of the giant cube would be identical to the other five faces. You could turn the cube 1/4-turn and it would look exactly the same as before you turned it. You would also be able to split the giant cube along 999 parallel planes, between each of the tiny blocks. But because we can't tell one face from another, we can't tell one parallel set of cleavage planes from another. This is a little tricky to get your mind around, but it will make sense as you start to see it in real minerals. Two good examples of this are galena and calcite. Galena is a cubic mineral exactly like the example we've described above; it is formed from gazillions of tiny, little cube shapes, and it cleaves perfectly into little cubes. Each face looks the same as every other face, so we say that galena has <u>one</u> cleavage. Calcite also has one perfect cleavage, but it has three-sided symmetry instead of four-sided symmetry. A broken crystal of calcite shows what look like somewhat squashed, three-sided pyramids. These are called rhombohedrons (rhombs, for short).

Mineral Profile: Mica

Mica, like feldspar, is actually the name of a family of minerals. Unlike the feldspars, these are much easier to recognize both generally and specifically. Micas all split easily and perfectly into plates and sheets; with patience and care, you can split some into sheets thinner than paper. Often, people have a hard time believing these are minerals—they seem more like a plastic film.

The two most common micas are muscovite and biotite. The first is silvery-gray, and its thin sheets are nearly transparent. Sometimes it's referred to as "white mica." Biotite is nearly black, and isn't nearly as transparent as muscovite. Logically, it's sometimes called "black mica." A rare variety rich in lithium is called lepidolite, and is colored a beautiful pink to lavender. Chlorite is a green variety, which isn't visible as crystals very often, but it's common and abundant as *microscopic* crystals that can give a green cast to clay, soils, igneous rocks, and especially fine- to medium-grained foliated metamorphic rocks (slates to schists). You will notice that in the mineral data, the "stats" are much more variable than normal; this is due to the variety of different micas.

Science Fair Extensions

26.   Using a thick piece of mica, demonstrate the ability to cleave it along a parallel plane. Split the mica as many times as you can and then display the product of your energies.

27.   Cleavage and fracture are also very important to gemologists. Find out how diamonds, rubies, emeralds, and other rare and precious gems are cut and prepared. Note some of the hazards of gem-cutting, as well as the benefits.

Acid Test

Geologically Speaking ...

Dilute acetic acid is known as household vinegar. It's the same stuff that you use to make Italian salad dressing and to dye Easter eggs. Vinegar reacts when it comes in contact with calcium carbonate by producing carbon dioxide gas. When this happens, small bubbles of gas appear on the surface of the mineral or rock being tested.

The fizz or acid test is a check for a mineral that contains carbonate. Calcite is a mineral made of calcium carbonate. The acid attacks the mineral immediately, releasing carbon dioxide and literally dissolving the mineral.

Materials

8   Mineral samples (amethyst, azurite, calcite, lodestone, mica, rose quartz, talc, pyrite)
1   Bottle of vinegar (dilute acetic acid)
1   Cup
1   Eyedropper
1   Hand lens
1   Steel nail
1   Paper towel

Procedure

1. Pour a little vinegar into a cup, so that the vinegar can be picked up with the dropper.

2. To test a mineral sample for a reaction with the vinegar, place two drops of vinegar on the surface of the mineral and use the hand lens to determine if bubbles appear. If they do, write *yes* in the *Fizz* column in your data table. If no bubbles appear after about 15 seconds, then write *no*.

3. Wipe the sample dry with a paper towel. Test the hardness of the rock with the nail (see the Hardness Test section, if you're not sure about this one). If the sample is harder than the nail, you will see a steel-gray streak on the sample. Write *too hard* in the *Powder* column. If the sample is softer than the nail, it will powder up a little as you scratch at it. Put two drops of vinegar onto the powder. Again, examine the wetted surface with your lens and look for bubbles. Write *yes* or *no* to show whether or not you saw bubbles from the powder.

Data & Observations

Record your observations in the data table below.

Sample Name	Fizz (yes/no)	Powder (yes/no/too hard)
1._____	_____	_____
2._____	_____	_____
3._____	_____	_____
4._____	_____	_____
5._____	_____	_____
6._____	_____	_____
7._____	_____	_____
8._____	_____	_____

How Come, Huh?

If the sample fizzed, it is probably calcite (if crystals are visible) or limestone (if individual crystals are not visible). If the <u>powder</u> fizzed, but the unscratched rock did not, it is probably dolomite. Dolomite is similar to calcite, but has some magnesium in place of some of the calcium. Magnesium bonds tighter than calcium, so the sample won't fizz as easily. Other carbonate minerals will also show bubbles in the acid test, but calcite and dolomite are the two most common and abundant. Frequently, the difference between their "fizzability" is the only way to tell which one you have, without sophisticated testing.

Acid Test

Mineral Profile: Calcite

Calcite is a very common and abundant mineral that can show up just about anywhere. Its major components are calcium oxide, which is present in most rocks, and carbon dioxide, which is a significant part of the atmosphere. So calcite forms regularly as calcium-bearing rocks weather. Calcite, or a similar mineral called aragonite, also forms the hard parts of many marine animals, such as mollusks (clams, oysters, snails, and so on), corals, microscopic critters called coccoliths, and many others. When these animals die, their skeletons can accumulate on the sea floor and eventually harden into limestone.

When you put acid onto calcite, what you're actually doing is dissolving the calcium into the acid and releasing carbon dioxide back into the air. We think of carbon as residing mostly in living things, but the fact is that more than 99% of the carbon in the Earth system is tied up as calcite or similar minerals.

Calcite is most commonly transparent or milky-white when in crystals large enough to see, but it is one of the most variable minerals in terms of color. It exists in all colors of the rainbow. Transparent crystals show a marvelous optical effect called double refraction, where an image seen though the crystal is split in two.

Science Fair Extensions

28. Collect samples of different kinds of limestones and determine a method for gauging the amount of calcium carbonate present in each kind of rock.

Magnetism Tests

Geologically Speaking ...

A select group of minerals will produce a magnetic field under the right conditions. The most common of these is an iron-rich mineral called magnetite. The test to determine if a mineral is magnetic is to dip it into a pile of iron filings. If the mineral produces a magnetic field, it will attract and pick up the filings and deflect the needle of a compass.

It is much more common for a mineral to be attracted to a magnet than it is for a mineral to actually produce an observable magnetic field. But both properties are useful and related, so you're going to get two tests for the price of one here.

Materials

8   Mineral samples (amethyst, azurite, calcite, lodestone, mica, rose quartz, talc, pyrite)
1   Bottle of iron filings
1   Baggie
1   Pie tin

Procedure 1

1. Pour a small amount of iron filings into the pie tin. Take mineral sample #1 and place it in the baggie.

2. Lower the baggie so that the mineral sample comes in contact with the iron filings. If it is magnetic, it will attract the iron filings through the baggie and the mineral will appear to have a brown beard. If it is non-magnetic, the iron filings will remain in the bottom of the tin.

3. Remove the sample from the baggie, and the filings will drop back into the pie tin.

Magnetism Tests

More Materials

8   Mineral samples (same as on page 99)
1   Bar magnet, 1 inch long
1   Piece of string, about 3 feet long
1   Tack

Procedure 2

1. Tie a small loop in one end of the string. Tie the magnet to the other end.

2. Tack the string and magnet up so that the magnet hangs at the end of the string. A doorframe is good for this, or you could skip the tack, tape the string to something, and hang it over the edge of a table. Allow the magnet a minute or so to stop swinging and spinning.

3. Gently bring a sample to within a 1/2-inch or so of the magnet. If there are minerals in the sample that are attracted to magnetic fields, you will see the magnet move, either swinging toward the sample or turning one end toward the sample. This is a very sensitive test. If you have a sample of granite with tiny sand-grain-sized black spots, test the black spots. Often, they're magnetite, but they're not big enough to give a positive test for Procedure 1.

Data & Observations

Record your observations in the data table on the next page. If you got a positive test on the first procedure, write *yes* in the *Magnetic Field?* column; on the second procedure, write *yes* in the last column. A *yes* on the *Magnetic Field?* column means you probably have a substantial amount of magnetite. In the last column, a *yes* indicates a small amount of magnetite or other magnetically-attractive mineral, such as pyrrhotite.

Sample/Color		Magnetic Field?	Magnetically Attractive?
1	Purple	_____	_____
2	Blue	_____	_____
3	White	_____	_____
4	Gray	_____	_____
5	Silver	_____	_____
6	Pink	_____	_____
7	Green	_____	_____
8	Gold	_____	_____

Mineral Profile: Lodestone

Lodestone is the name of a mineral that has a strong magnetic field. If you tie a sample of lodestone onto a string and let it hang freely, it will consistently turn to a certain position. This is the result of the stone aligning its own mag-netic field to the Earth's magnetic field. While lodestone is the common name for this mineral, it is called magnetite by geologists.

Magnetism Tests

Mineral Profile: Lodestone

Magnetite doesn't necessarily have a strong magnetic field, but it will always be attracted to a magnet. You can use this characteristic not only to see if magnetite is present, but also to concentrate grains of this mineral. When you see streaks of darker sand at a beach or river shore, run a magnet through the dark areas. Magnetite will stick to the magnet, giving it a beard. Wipe the beard off into a container (film cannisters are good for this kind of stuff), and repeat as desired to get a good collection of grains.

Magnetite is an important ore of iron. Because of its magnetic properties, an important prospecting technique involves looking at anomolies, or variations, in Earth's magnetic field. Some other minerals, such as pyrrhotite, also display magnetism, but none are as strongly magnetic, common, or abundant, as magnetite.

Science Fair Extensions

29. Compare a free-hanging piece of magnetite with the readings that you get from a compass. Mark and place the magnetite in three different locations and compare the orientation of the magnetite with the compass reading you take.

Big Idea 5

Extrusive igneous rocks are formed when molten rock, called lava, erupts from a volcano onto the surface of the Earth and solidifies.

Volcano Q & A

What Exactly is a Volcano?

A volcano is an opening in the crust of the Earth that produces hot, liquid magma, ash, and gas. It can be a pile of lava anywhere from a small cone, like an eruption in Hawaii, to a huge, 23,000-foot mountain perched in the Andes of South America.

What Causes a Volcano to Erupt?

Too much pressure causes a volcano to erupt. Magma under the surface of the Earth is constantly moving and squishing around. Imagine sitting on a tube of toothpaste, and you get the general idea. If conditions are right, magma creates so much pressure under a specific portion of the crust that the only way to relieve that pressure is for the magma under the surface to explode out onto the Earth.

How Many Volcanos Are There in the World?

There are somewhere between 1,500 and 1,800 volcanos, depending on whom you talk to. Most are dormant, which means they are asleep but not dead. Depending on conditions, they may come to life every couple hundred to thousand years or so. If a volcano is extinct, it has already erupted in the past but will not erupt again. If a volcano is active and you are near it, you should pack the car and make like Mario Andretti.

Where Do These Rocks Come From?

Many volcanic rocks come from a region in Northern California, called the Medicine Lake Highland. The Highland is a giant shield volcano. Think of it as a pancake. It is spread out over a wide area and there are lots of holes (vents) visible in the surface. Because it is a large volcano, spread over a large area, with lots of vents, there are lots of different kinds of eruptions, cracks, fissures, and opportunities for unique rocks to form, cool, and wait to be discovered by you and me.

You might want to find a geological map of the Medicine Lake Highland. The different patterns, dots, bars, and white areas represent different lava flows that erupted at different times. The numbers followed by M are elevation readings in meters. Other features like vents and craters are identified on the map, as are faults, represented by lines with cross-hatchings through them.

This volcanic area is very unique and rare in the number and different kinds of rocks that it forms. If you are interested in digging into this topic deeper, nab a copy of our kit, *Fire on the Mountain*.

Oozeology 101

Geologically Speaking ...

Not all lavas are created equal. One of the main ingredients in a batch of lava is **silica**. Glass. The same stuff that sand is made from. Lavas that have a lot of silica are sticky, thick, and flow slowly. Lava that does not have a lot of silica is runny, flows easily, and oozes all over the place during an eruption.

Iron-rich volcanic glass is very high in silica—about 90%, to be exact. When this silica-rich lava cools, the rock takes on a glassy texture, fractures like glass when it is dropped, and also has <u>very sharp edges</u>, just like glass. Be careful with this rock.

Materials

1   1 oz. bottle of sodium tetraborate
1   1 oz. bottle of polyvinyl alcohol
1   1 mL pipette
1   5 oz. wax cup
1   Craft stick
1   Sample of obsidian

Procedure

1. Empty the entire bottle of polyvinyl alcohol into the wax cup. If you stick your finger in the cup and touch the chemical inside, you will find a pile of long, sticky polymers that feel slippery to the touch.

2. Remove the cap from the sodium tetraborate and insert the skinny end of the pipette. Squeeze the bulb and release, filling the pipette to the 1 mL mark. That is the top of four lines on the tube of the pipette. Add the milliliter of sodium tetraborate to the polyvinyl alcohol in the cup. Add a second milliliter to the cup. Replace the cap on the bottle.

3. Using the craft stick, stir the two chemicals together. As you stir, they will begin forming lots and lots of connections to produce a big, slippery net of molecules. When the consistency reaches a slimy texture, pull it out of the cup and play with it.

4. Put the ooze back into the cup and find a smooth, hard surface, like a table or countertop. Tip the cup over onto the hard surface and observe what happens to the ooze that you have produced. Imagine that this is how iron-rich volcanic glass moves once it escapes from the vent of the volcano.

5. When you are done with this experiment, scoop the ooze back into the cup and save it, or you can toss it into the garbage.

Data & Observations

On the lines below, describe how the ooze and an obsidian flow might be the same: _____

_____

_____

_____

_____

_____

STIR

CRAFT STICK

2 ML SODIUM TETRABORATE

1 OZ. POLYVINYL ALCOHOL

5 OZ. WAX CUP

Oozeology 101

How Come, Huh?

Iron-rich volcanic glass typically oozes from a crack or opening on the side of a volcano. Because it has lots of silica dissolved in its mix, it moves very slowly, like cold maple syrup covering a pancake.

When you pick your sample up, you might be able to see through the edges. This is because the black color, which is produced by the presence of iron, is not spread evenly through the lava. When it cools, some of the lava is clear rather than black. Some kinds of glass are red; this is because the iron in the magma had a chance to oxidize, or rust, before it solidified. Other kinds of glass have impurities that form discs, and others form spheres, but we'll save that for another time.

Rock Profile: Obsidian

How Was It Formed?

Obsidian is formed from a kind of lava called **rhyolite (rye • oh • light)** which contains a lot of silica, the material used to make glass. In fact, if you ever have the opportunity to walk across an obsidian or pumice deposit, it sounds like you are walking over a field of broken glass. Because rhyolite is a thick, sticky kind of lava, this flow oozed from the ground slowly. It also cooled quickly, which prevented large crystals from forming and contributes to the glassy appearance. The black color is produced by the presence of iron and is spread unevenly throughout the lava. If you hold your specimen up to a bright light, you may see that some areas of the sample are very dark and others are almost transparent. If your sample has streaks of red, this is iron that has oxidized (rusted). Such a unique sample is named mahogany obsidian.

What's It Used For?

Another name for obsidian is volcanic glass. If you hold a thin section of your sample up to the light, you can usually see light coming through portions of the rock. Because it could be chipped and shaped, the Indians used obsidian to make spears, arrowheads, and other war party favors. Today, high-quality surgical blades are made using obsidian because it holds a sharp, clean edge and does not produce as much scarring as metal blades ... had Custer only known.

Where Can I Find It?

Regions of volcanic activity are the best places to start. Most western states have several locations where obsidian deposits can be found.

Science Fair Extensions

30. Acquire several pieces of obsidian and do a little research to see how the Native Americans napped the rock to form arrowheads, spearheads, and scraping and skinning tools. Take a little time to make this work and you will have a great appreciation for the time and energy that went into this endeavor.

31. There are several kinds of obsidian. In addition to the plain, old, black obsidian that we described here, there is also mahogany obsidian, snowflake obsidian, gold sheen obsidian, pin fire obsidian, spherulitic obsidian, and even green obsidian that was created when flying lava coated pine trees in Northern California hundreds of years ago. Do some research and find out where these different kinds of obsidian can be found and why they have the properites that they do.

Rusty Rocks

Geologically Speaking ...

Try this lab to understand how iron is diffused in the lava to produce the basic black color that you see in all specimens, and also to understand the process that causes iron to **oxidize (ox • uh • dies)** and produce the red colors found in some specimens.

Materials

1   Steel wool pad (non-soap variety)
    Water
1   Tart pan
1   India ink
1   8 oz. glass
1   Sample of volcanic cinders

Procedure

1.   Fill the glass with water.

2.   Place one drop of black India ink in the glass and observe how it diffuses through the water. You will see patterns start to form as the heavier ink flows toward the bottom of the glass. The iron present in obsidian shows similar patterns.

3.   The steel wool should be the kind that is found in the paint section of a hardware store and that does not have any soap. 00000 grade is best. Soak the piece of steel wool in the glass of water. Squeeze out the excess water and place the pad in the tart pan. Leave it overnight and observe the changes the next day.

WATER

STEEL WOOL

TART PAN

Data & Observations

Draw a picture of the diffused black ink in the space that is provided below.

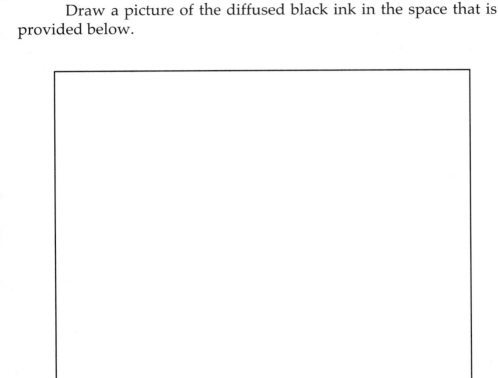

How Come, Huh?

The water reacts with the iron in the presence of oxygen to produce iron oxide (rust). If your sample of cinder has rust-colored streaks, compare the color to the rust in the steel wool. You will see that the colors are about the same. As the lava cooled and solidified, some of the iron oxidized and colored the normally-black cinders.

Rusty Rocks

Rock Profile: Volcanic Cinder

How Was It Formed?

This rock is commonly referred to as a lava rock and is one of the pyroclastic rocks you'll use. The word **pyroclastic** literally means "fire fragment," which gives you a clue as to why you shouldn't try to catch a fresh specimen right out of the vent. When hot, sticky lava erupts from a volcanic vent, it is ejected, or spit, into the air. As these blobs of hot lava fall back to Earth, they cool  very rapidly, trapping steam and other gases inside the rock. The end-product is a small, twisted (physically, not psychologically) rock with lots of holes in it—frothy pieces of basalt, if you will. These pile up as the vent continues to spit them out, and they eventually form a cinder cone. If it is an active cone, it can pile cinders several thousand feet high. Shastina, on the side of Mt. Shasta in Northern California, is a great example of this.

Lava that forms these volcanic cinders is less rich in silica than the lava that produces pumice, obsidian and andesite. It also contains minerals, like hornblende, which are rich in iron and magnesium. They contribute to the distinctive reddish-brown color produced as the iron and magnesium slowly oxidize (rust) over time.

What's It Used For?

There are a great number of cinder cones in Oregon, California, and Idaho. They are quarried for commercial purposes. Cinders are regularly used in road construction to provide a stable road base. In fact, some highways in Central Oregon are paved entirely with cinders and are famous for their red color. Cinders are also used for decorative rock borders in landscaping. Finally, if you look in the bottom of your barbecue, you might see cinders that catch the fat and give your Porterhouse a tasty flavor.

Where Can I Find It?

An excellent display of over 40 cinder cones can be found in Craters of the Moon National Monument in Idaho. You can also find cinders at Sunset Crater National Monument in Arizona, throughout Central Oregon, near Albuquerque, New Mexico, in the Aleutian Islands of Alaska, in California all along the eastern side of the Sierra Nevada Mountains, and all over Hawaii.

Science Fair Extensions

32. Experiment using different temperatures of water. Compare the rates of diffusion as you place the same number of drops of ink into the glass.

33. Create artificial lava (see the Lava Races lab) and then design an experiment to demonstrate how the red (oxidized iron) color could have been diffused through the magma as it flowed from the vent.

34. Repeat the second half of the Rusty Rocks experiment using the steel wool, but this time, place the wet steel wool inside a soda pop bottle, partially inflate a balloon, and insert the balloon over the opening of the bottle. Let the reaction stand for 24 hours and then observe what happened to the gas inside the balloon. Do a little research to learn why this reaction happened.

Styrofoam Rock

Geologically Speaking ...

Not all pumice is formed explosively. Sometimes the lava will ooze out of the vent, and away from it. As the lava leaves the vent, the pressure holding the water dissolved in the lava is released, and the water starts to turn into steam, forming bubbles in the lava flow. If the lava solidifies before the bubbles pop and the lava has a rhyolite composition, the rock that forms is a type of pumice. If this happens with a basaltic lava, it's called scoria. Either way, it's a foamy, lightweight rock.

Materials

1   1 oz. bottle polyurethane A
1   1 oz. bottle polyurethane B
1   Craft stick
1   9 oz. disposable plastic cup
1   Tart pan
1   Sample of pumice

Procedure

1.   We recommend that you do this experiment in a well-ventilated area, or outdoors, and avoid snorting the fumes. Put the plastic cup in the tart pan. Empty the entire bottle of polyurethane A into the cup; then empty the entire bottle of polyurethane B into the same cup.

2.   Take the craft stick and stir the two solutions together thoroughly. You will see an amber-colored solution that looks like spun honey. Toss the stick into the garbage and set the cup in the tart pan.

STIR

CRAFT STICK

1 OZ. POLY A

1 OZ. POLY B

5 OZ. WAX CUP

3. Touch the bottom side of the cup every 10 seconds. You should notice the temperature start to increase. Peek inside the cup and check the foam level each time you check the temperature. After about 60 seconds, the reaction really gets going and the two liquids produce a gas that is trapped in the warm, sticky liquid. This material is the foam polyurethane that is a common part of so many products in our world.

4. The foam will continue to billow up and will spill over the sides of the cup. DO NOT TOUCH THE FOAM. When the polyurethane is first forming, it is very sticky and hot and will leave a residue on your fingers. You can touch the side of the cup and feel the heat that is produced. This is called an **exothermic,** or heat-producing, reaction.

5. The polyurethane will cool quickly, and you will be able to push, whap, and thump on the foam, once it has been left to harden for a few minutes. When you are finished looking at the foam, it's yours to keep.

Styrofoam Rock

Data & Observations

Draw a picture of the way poly A and poly B looked right after you mixed them. Then draw what the solution looked like.

How Come, Huh?

This is the same way that a non-violent eruption of a volcano can produce pumice. As pressure is released from the lava, dissolved gases (particularly water vapor, in the case of lava) bubble out and make the lava foamy. When the lava hardens, the foam is trapped in the solid rock.

This also does a pretty god job of showing how a dome-building eruption takes place. In a real dome-building eruption, the upper surface of the extruded lava is pretty solid, but the material at the vent still flows a little. The landform created is called a dome; it looks like the top of a muffin rising out of a muffin tin as it cooks. In this experiment, we created a dome of polyurethane. In a real eruption, a dome of rhyolite or andesite might be created. The later eruptions of Mount St. Helens were dome-building eruptions, and the dome created by those eruptions is now observable from the nearby Visitors' Center. For a little insight into what can happen if pressure builds up under the dome, see Dome Explosions. To see what happens if the magma solidfies before it leaves the vent, see Burnt Sugar Snakes.

Rock Profile: Pumice

How Was It Formed?

You wouldn't know by looking at them, but obsidian and pumice start out in-side the Earth as exactly the same kind of molten lava, rhyolite. Pumice is just frothy obsidian. Rhyolite is a thick, sticky lava, so it tends to just sit in the neck of the volcanic vent like a big gooey cork. This blocks the opening of the volcano, and if more lava wants to get out, the pressure inside the volcano increases. So, when the volcano finally blows, it really explodes, sending molten pieces of pumice, called pyroclasts, flying for miles. Bad news for local picnicers!

Styrofoam Rock

The difference between obsidian and pumice as far as texture, color, and density go is due to one small variable. When the magma was created deep inside the Earth, it mixed with a lot of water. Chance coincidence, poor planning on the part of the volcano vent committee…, doesn't matter; it mixed with the water and that drastically changed the behavior of the molten rock. As this water-rich, superheated lava erupted from the vent, the water flashed to steam. This produced zillions of small gas holes, as the steam got trapped in the rapidly cooling rock. The boiling water also mangled the texture of the rock, whipping it into a frothy hot liquid. The cooled lava, filled with all of the steam voids, was very light—so light it could float on water. Hence, pumice was born.

What's It Used For?
Crushed pumice is used as an abrasive material in cleansing and scouring products, including my dad's favorite brand of hand soap, "Lava." Ideal if your objective is complete skin removal. Chunks of pumice are used to remove callouses on feet and rings on toilets and bathtubs. In the early days of Hollywood, while polymer science was still waiting to be discovered, large pieces of pumice were used as "strong man" props.

Where Can I Find It?
Pumice can be found in areas of volcanic activity, particularly near Crater Lake National Park in Oregon. There are several hundred square miles east of the park littered with chunks of pumice. It is not uncommon in the spring to find "rock" floating downstream as the snows melt. At least it is consistent with the state travel guide, which boasts, *"Things look different out here."*

Science Fair Extensions
35. Repeat the experiment using hot and cold poly A and B and see how the rates of reaction are affected.

Volcanic Popcorn

Geologically Speaking ...

This lab will demonstrate the similarities between the formation of pumice from water-rich rhyolitic magma and the formation of popcorn from a water-rich popcorn kernel.

As we mentioned, it is believed that pumice is formed when hot lava, mixed with large quantities of water, erupts. As the magma exits the vent, the water boils and turns to steam. In fact, chemists have determined that when water does turn to steam, it expands to 1800 times its original volume. This rapid expansion cools the pumice and produces rock that is much *less dense* than it was originally. Popcorn kernels also have a small bit of water in them. As they are heated, the water expands rapidly, creating so much pressure that the husk bursts and the popcorn is cooked. Very similar to pumice but easier on the teeth!

Materials

1   Bag of popcorn kernels
2   Tablespoons of cooking oil
1   Qt. pan (with lid)
1   Stove or hot plate
    or
1   Bag of microwave popcorn
1   Microwave oven
    and
1   Metric ruler
1   Sharpened pencil
1   Piece of pumice
1   Piece of obsidian
1   Glass of water
1   Sample of popcorn bomb

Volcanic Popcorn

Procedure

1. Take a loose kernel of unpopped popcorn and place it in the center of the first box on the next page. Using a very sharp pencil, trace around the kernel. Try to make the tracing as close to the kernel's *exact* shape as possible.

2. Using your metric ruler, measure the width and length of the kernel and record those measurements, to the nearest millimeter, in the space provided under the box.

3. Drop the unpopped popcorn kernel into the glass of water and observe whether it sinks or floats.

4. Make a batch of popcorn using either the traditional (and some would contend, far superior) method of heating a pan of oil over a stove and adding popcorn, or the more convenient microwave method, which relies more on finger pressure than intuitive culinary skills. Take a sample of the popped popcorn and place it in the second box on the next page. Trace, measure, and record the data in the appropriate space. Don't forget the sink / float test.

5. Finally, compare the obsidian to the pumice in the buoyancy department, as well as the color and hardness departments. Because both are made of similar lava material, rhyolitic magma, we challenge you to decide which one represents the unpopped kernel and which one represents the popped popcorn.

How Come, Huh?

This is the same way that a violent eruption of a volcano can produce pumice as well as pyroclasts. As pressure is released from the lava, dissolved gases (particularly water vapor in the case of lava) bubble out and make the lava foamy. As this hot, gooey lava shoots through the air, it expands, stretches, and continues to cool. Evidence of all three activities can be seen on the surface of the bomb. It is very light, and air bubbles are visible. The stretching of the lava is evident by the lines on the sides of the bomb. It cooled before it hits the ground or it would be deformed on one side.

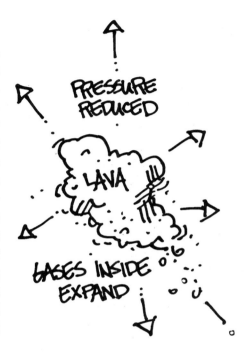

Data & Observations

Draw a picture of the unpopped kernel / popped popcorn in the spaces that are provided below.

Unpopped kernel: _____ mm   Popped kernel: _____ mm

Volcanic Popcorn

Rock Profile: Popcorn Rhyolite Bomb

This is a very light rock that has swirled bands of dark and light color. Some of the specimens have what appears to be a glazed coating on the surface. Some are so light that they can float in water.

How Was It Formed?

This rock started out as a glob of glass-rich, molten lava full of dissolved gas stuck in the neck of a cinder cone. When the cinder cone erupted, shooting globs of hot molten lava through the air, three things were happening at virtually the same time:

1. The gas that was dissolved in the glob of lava started to expand very rapidly, producing thousands of tiny holes, just like a popcorn kernel popping open.

2. At the same time, the outside of the bomb was cooling very quickly, forming a hard shell.

3. As this still-gooey glob was shooting through the air, expanding on the inside and hardening on the outside, gravity and the friction of the air moving past the glob was tugging and twisting the lava, forming the beautiful patterns you see on the outside of the bomb.

Geo Factoids

Bread crust bombs have also been found on Echo Mountain. These are formed when the interior of the bomb continues to expand after the outside has produced a hard shell. The pressure against the shell causes it to crack open, so it looks like a loaf of bread.

What's It Used For?

These specimens are so rare that they are usually found only in collections.

Where Can I Find It?
Northern California.

Science Fair Extensions

36. Do some digging and find a good French bread recipe. Mix the dough (lava), place it in the oven (volcano), measure its volume, then let it bake for the appropriate amount of time. Observe the surface of the bread (breadcrust bomb) and compare its volume with its original size.

37. Compare the previous experiment that uses poly A and poly B to create the new compound with this experiment that uses popcorn. Cite the similarities and differences between the two experiments and explain which one provides a better model of origination and why.

Elephant Skin Sorbet

Geologically Speaking ...

You have probably noticed that a lot of volcanic rocks have bubbles in them. The bubbles are the by-products of dissolved gas and water that boils once the lava erupts onto the surface of the Earth.

Sometimes the lava does not make it all the way out of the vent. The lava that coats the side of the vent is heated and then cools, and is then reheated with the next explosion, so it undergoes a lot of violent changes. This experiment will give you an idea of how a rock with lots of holes could be formed.

Materials

1   7/8 oz. bottle of aluminum sulfate
    powder
1   7/8 oz. bottle of sodium bicarbonate
       powder
1   1 oz. bottle of liquid detergent
1   5 oz. wax cup
1   Craft stick
1   Toobe
1   Tart pan, 5 inches in diam.
1   Sample of andesite

Procedure

1. Add three ounces of water to the wax cup. Remove the cap from the bottle of aluminum sulfate powder. Fill the cap with powder and empty the powder into the wax cup.

2. Stir the powder until it has all dissolved, and empty the contents of the wax cup into the Toobe.

3. Rinse the wax cup with water and repeat Step 1 using the sodium bicarbonate powder. This time, add a dash of liquid detergent to the cup after you have stirred all of the powder into solution.

BAKING SODA SOLUTION

ALUMINUM SULFATE SOLUTION + SOAP

TOOBE

4. Place the Toobe in the center of the tart pan. Time for the "eruption." Slowly add the baking soda solution to the aluminum sulfate. As the two chemicals react with each other, they will produce large quantities of carbon dioxide gas. This gas will be trapped in the liquid because the detergent provides strength to the walls of the bubbles. As the number of gas bubbles increases, the bubbles run out of room near the surface of the liquid and start to push the bubbles that were formed at the bottom up and out of the Toobe.

5. If you examine the foam in the neck of the Toobe, you will see that it has lots of bubbles, just like your featherweight vent foam. You can also see that some of the bubbles are burst or damaged in the eruption. The same thing happens in a volcanic vent.

Why'd We Do This?

This is similar to what happened in the volcanic vent to form the featherweight vent foam. The reaction between the two liquids produced a gas that expanded and oozed up and out of the Toobe. The gas bubbles got trapped in this liquid and produced a cavity, or hole, in the finished product.

Elephant Skin Sorbet

"Why the name?," you ask. If you ever have an opportunity to see lava flow, from the air, you would notice that the ridges and layers in the lava look like the wrinkles you see around the joints of an elephant.

Rock Profile: Andesite

How Was It Formed?

Andesite is the kind of lava that Mama Bear would love. It's not too thick; it's not too runny. The color is not too dark and it's not too light, and did we mention that the silica content was just right? This kind of lava is produced when two pieces of the Earth's crust, called **tectonic (teck • tawn • ick) plates**, collide with each other. Particularly,  with andesite, if an ocean plate bumps into a land plate, something has to give. The ocean plate usually gets crammed underneath the land plate and starts to melt as it goes inside the Earth. This collision is not easy on the continental plate either, because it gets cracked. Some of the melted ocean plate oozes up through the cracks, melting and mixing with other kinds of rocks, producing andesite, a mixture of rocks from the two plates.

The magma, trapped in the volcano's chamber, starts to cool and allow *some* of the minerals to become large enough to be seen with the naked eye. Usually, the rest of the surrounding material is made up of minerals too small to be seen without magnification. The reason is that part way through this cooling inside the volcano, the whole mess erupted. Once outside the volcano, the remainder of the lava cooled very rapidly, and crystal growth was discouraged.

This type of rock, with two distinct sizes of crystals, is called a **porphyry (poor • free)**. It's like a chocolate chip cookie. The chips are the minerals that are large enough to be seen with the naked eye, and the rest of the cookie represents the minerals that are too small to be seen without magnification.

Where Can I Find It?

Anywhere along the "Ring of Fire," an extremely long band of volcanos that surrounds the Pacific Ocean. It begins in the Andes Mountains of Argentina, where it got its name, by the way, and continues through Mexico into Canada, curling around into the Aleutian Islands of Alaska. Then, it goes over to Japan and down through Indonesia, ending in the South Pacific. One heck of a field trip.

Science Fair Extensions

38. Compare the appearance of elephant skin, especially around the joints, with the appearance of lava flows. Note the similarities and differences.

Dome Explosions

Geologically Speaking ...

You will add vinegar to the bottom of a test tube. Then baking soda that has been wrapped in a piece of toilet paper is inserted into the top of the tube, where it remains. The whole assembly is stoppered and shaken. As the two chemicals react, the stopper is pushed out of the tube very quickly. Some would even go so far as to call it an explosion.

STOPPER

BAKING SODA IN TOILET PAPER

VINEGAR

TEST TUBE

Materials

1   16 mm x 150 mm test tube
1   #1 rubber stopper, solid
1   1 oz. bottle of white, distilled vinegar
1   Sheet of toilet paper
1   Bottle of baking soda powder
1   Sample of breccia

Procedure

1. Take a single section of toilet paper and pour a pile of baking soda roughly the size of a quarter onto it. Fold the toilet paper in half several times until it looks something like a plug.

2. Hold the test tube in one hand and pour about half an inch of vinegar into the bottom of it.

3. Insert the toilet paper plug into the *top* of the tube, and shove it in with the rubber stopper. Be sure you are pointing the stoppered end of the tube *toward* the ceiling and *away* from other kids.

4. While pointing the tube *away* from yourself and others, shake the tube vigorously several times. There will be a very quick chemical reaction inside the tube, and the stopper will explode into the air. *Be sure you are pointing the tube up and away from other kids.*

How Come, Huh?

Quite often, an active volcano will produce a dome inside its vent. This dome acts like a plug, similar to the stopper in the tube. When the pressure inside the volcano builds up, it eventually causes the dome to explode, shattering it into the air. This build-up of pressure inside the volcano is one of the main reasons that andesitic volcanos are so destructive when they erupt.

Rock Profile: Volcanic Breccia

How Was It Formed?

When a volcanic eruption has a lot of gas, fragments and blobs of the sticky lava tend to get thrown away from the vent and form a hot pile. If the blobs are still sticky or molten, their edges will fuse together, forming a solid rock composed of pyroclasts. This type of rock is called **volcanic breccia (bre-chuh).**

Dome Explosions

Rock Profile: Volcanic Breccia

Even if the blobs are too cool to stick together, they may be cemented during burial, as ground water deposits minerals between the fragments. This would still be called a volcanic breccia.

The term breccia refers to the broken nature of the fragments of rock. It does not really say anything about *how* the rock fragments got broken. In the case of volcanic breccia, we are saying the rock was formed and fragmented by volcanic activity. Other types of breccia include fault breccia (rocks get pulverized and broken when two fault blocks grind past each other), sedimentary breccia (rocks get broken during erosional transport, but aren't carried far enough to round their corners), landslide breccia (rocks slide down a mountain and end up in a pile that is later cemented together), and impact breccia (an exotic type formed by meteorite impacts—rare on Earth, but covers much of the moon and various other bodies in our solar system.)

So how would you know that a particular rock was a volcanic breccia rather than some other type? First, look at the fragments that make up the rock. If they are nearly all the same kind of material and if that material looks like volcanic rock, volcanic breccia is an excellent first guess. Second, look at how the fragments are cemented into a single rock. If their edges appear to be melted together, the rock is almost certainly volcanic breccia.

Science Fair Extensions

39. Build an entire mountain with clay or papier mache around a glass that you place in the center of a pie tin. As you build the model, decide how much of the mountain is actually going to be blown away, and construct a removable piece. Erupt your volcano, and as the reaction subsides, remove a piece, showing how the mountain was destroyed. Be prepared to discuss the formation of Crater Lake, Mt. St. Helens, and other volcanos.

40. The experiment that explains how to make coquina, Coquina Macaroni, also gives you an idea of how this rock is formed.

Burnt Sugar Snakes

Geologically Speaking ...

Sometimes, volcanic eruptions don't push lava out of the ground in the strict sense of the word lava. Lava means molten rock on the Earth's surface, but the molten rock in the volcano's vent (which technically would be called magma) can solidify before it has a chance to reach the surface. But even this solid rock can be forced out of the vent if the pressure underneath it is high enough. This would be called a plug-building or dome-building eruption, depending on what form the extruding rock takes. In a plug eruption, a spire of solid rock simply rises up out of the vent, towering as much as hundreds of feet in the air. Sounds safe and simple, but if this tower of still-hot rock falls down, it can wreak havoc on anyone admiring the rock from below. Just such an event wiped out the town of Martinique, in the Caribbean, early last century. The one fellow who survived happened to have been locked up in the town jail, which, as luck would have it, was underground.

In this lab, you will see firsthand how a plug eruption would take place, along with lots of the nasty odors that go with it. THIS SHOULD BE PERFORMED IN A WELL-VENTILATED AREA OR OUTDOORS. THE SULFURIC ACID USED HERE IS VERY HAZ-ARDOUS TO SKIN, BONE, EYES, OR ANY OTHER PART OF YOUR BODY. WE RECOMMEND GOGGLES AND RUBBER GLOVES. HAVE PLENTY OF WA-TER IMMEDIATELY AVAILABLE TO DEAL WITH ACCIDENTAL CONTACT.

Actually, our preference is that this be done by a responsible adult, with young'uns looking on and taking copious notes.

Burnt Sugar Snakes

Materials

1 Bottle of concentrated sulfuric acid
1 Box of granulated sugar
1 100 mL beaker
1 Tart pan
2 Napkins or paper towels
1 Baggie
  Water (for safety purposes)
1 Sample of vesicular basalt

Procedure

1. Wet one napkin with water and place it on a clean, hard surface (we recommend a patio or driveway, outdoors). This will absorb most of the heat generated by the reaction. Flip the tart pan upside down and place it on the wet napkin.

2. Place the 100 mL beaker in the center of the tart pan and fill it to the 40 mL mark with granulated sugar.

3. Very carefully add 40 mL of concentrated sulfuric acid to the granulated sugar. The reaction may take a couple of minutes to really get going; then once it starts, it finishes in another two minutes or so. Keep an eye on it.

40 ML H$_2$SO$_4$

40 ML SUGAR

100 ML BEAKER

4. You will notice that the sugar turns brown pretty quickly, and then turns black. The sugar is literally being cooked by the reaction with the sulfuric acid, and a long black snake will grow out of the beaker, along with smoke and fumes. It will usually reach a length of four inches or so.

☆ **DO NOT INHALE THE FUMES.** THE GAS CONTAINS SULFURIC ACID, WHICH CAN REACT WITH TISSUES IN YOUR THROAT AND LUNGS. THIS GIVES YOU A VERY SORE THROAT.

☆ **DO NOT TOUCH THE SNAKE WITH YOUR BARE HANDS.** FIRST OF ALL, IT IS HOT, AND SECOND, IT HAS SULFURIC ACID IN IT.

5. When you are done and the snake has cooled (give it 5-10 minutes), you can wrap the snake in a second napkin, place it in a resealable baggie, and toss it into the trash. <u>Wash your hands.</u>

How Come, Huh?

Volcanos can erupt in a number of ways, and we want you to see a variety of those ways. This has some features in common with dome-building eruptions, and can also continue with a later explosion from gases trapped under the plug. By the way, the material solidifying in the vent is called a plug because it "plugs" the vent ... very clever, eh?

Burnt Sugar Snakes

Rock Profile: Basalt

How Was It Formed?

Basalt is the most common of all the volcanic rocks found on Earth and is typically formed when hot magma oozes through an opening in the crust. The cinders described on the previous page are a frothy version of basalt. Once outside, the hot lava cools very  quickly as it comes into contact with either the air or ocean water. This rapid cooling prevents minerals from growing large enough to form crystals that can be seen without magnification, which explains why your specimen appears to be a single, uniform color. Quite often (you'll see this in your specimen) the rapid cooling traps small bubbles of air, steam, or other gases. Like the pumice, this creates many holes, and the holes are a common characteristic of basalt.

Shield Volcanos

If the opening in the Earth is a volcanic vent in the middle of the ocean, then long, sloping, shield volcanos, like the Hawaiian Islands, are formed. When the lava from the islands' volcanos reaches the ocean, a great steam explosion occurs.

Basalt Pillows

Or, if the opening is under the sea, the lava spills out onto the ocean floor, forming pillow basalt. When geologists find pillow basalt on land, it indicates that the land was formed under water.

Basalt Floods

If the choice of exit is a fissure, or large crack in the ground, then the lava literally floods the countryside, coating it with layers and layers of lava, sometimes hundreds of feet thick.

Basalt Plugs

Occasionally, basalt will fill the vent of a volcano and solidify. Eventually, the soft, outer portion of the volcano erodes away, exposing the basalt. The Devil's Tower in Wyoming is an excellent example.

What's It Used for?

Basalt is a very abundant, inexpensive rock used for road base, paving, building materials, and railroad track grade. In the West during the 1800s, farmers and ranchers expended a great deal of effort clearing fields of basalt rocks and piling them into great fences running along their properties. Many of these still exist in Northern California. Farmers probably would have preferred cedar fencing, but you have to work with what the land provides.

Basalt columns along the Columbia River Gorge in the Pacific Northwest are used for recreational climbing. The rock is very hard, holds pitons and wedges well, and has enough cracks to provide finger- and toe-holds for anyone willing to climb a sheer wall of extrusive igneous rock.

Burnt Sugar Snakes

Rock Profile: Basalt

Where Can I Find It?

There are outcrops of basalt throughout the western United States. Some of the more notable ones are The Devil's Postpile in California, Devil's Tower in Wyoming, Columbia River Gorge National Scenic Area separating Oregon and Washington, and Black Rock Canyon and Paul Bunyan's Postpile in Utah. All of these areas demonstrate the hexagonal joints and columns that are quite often characteristic of basalt flows.

Large deposits can be found throughout the Pacific Northwest. Much of eastern Washington and Oregon are covered with basalt that oozed from the ground when fissures opened up, from time to time, beginning 15 million years ago. This opening spread "flood basalts" over the entire area. In some locations along the Columbia River Gorge, the basalt is 2,500 feet thick.

Idaho is home to a huge lava plain that extends over most of the southern portion of the state. Flooding produced an incredibly impressive and beautiful landscape that includes the Snake River Canyon, Craters of the Moon National Monument, and Hell's Canyon National Recreation Area.

Science Fair Extensions

41. Many kinds of lava have holes in their composition. Vesicular obsidian is quarried, cut, and used for grill blocks. There is vesicular basalt, vesicular cinders, and, of course, vesicular rhyolite, which is also called pumice. Compare the appearance of all three.

Dry Ice Ash Flows

Geologically Speaking ...

To understand how hot fragments of lava "ride" on gases and flow down the side of a volcano, we are going to use dry ice, which is solid carbon dioxide, to represent the gases produced by a volcano, and soap bubbles to represent the lava fragments.

Materials

1   10 gallon aquarium
2   Pounds of dry ice
1   Hammer
1   Bottle of bubble solution with wand
1   Pair of gloves (insulated gloves, not rubber gloves)
1   Cloth or paper bag
1   Sample of tuff or welded ash

Procedure

1. *Put on your insulated gloves (not rubber gloves)* and set the dry ice on a hard surface. Cover it with the cloth or paper bag and smash it into little pieces with the hammer. Again, with gloved hands, remove the cover, pick up the dry ice pieces, and place them in the aquarium. *Dry ice is 109 degrees Fahrenheit below zero. If you touch it with bare hands, you run the risk of freezing your skin cells solid, which tends to kill them instantly. Be safe and use the gloves.*

2. Allow the dry ice pieces to stand undisturbed for a couple of minutes. Dry ice is the solid form of carbon dioxide. At room temperature, dry ice undergoes a process called *sublimation*, changing directly from a solid to a gas. As you wait, the aquarium will fill up with this invisible carbon dioxide. Because carbon dioxide is heavier than air, it displaces the air, or pushes it up and out of the aquarium.

Dry Ice Ash Flows

3.   After two minutes, take the bubble solution and blow bubbles *over* the top of the aquarium so that they float down into it. Do not blow down into the aquarium or you will blow the gas out of the container. Observe the bubbles. The carbon dioxide is heavier than the air trapped in the bubbles, so the bubbles look like spheres bobbing up and down on an invisible ocean of gas.

4.   Fill the aquarium with bubbles and then gently tilt it at a 45 degree angle as shown below in the picture of our friend Pyro. The bubbles will "ride" on the heavier carbon dioxide gas, out of the aquarium and onto the floor. This is similar to the way that molten ash rides hot gases down the side of a volcano. When the molten ash gets to its final destination, it settles to the ground. If it is hot and sticky, it forms a soft, fragmented rock. If the ash cools and solidifies before it settles to the ground, it remains in individual pieces and looks like the sample that you will use in your next lab.

Data & Observations

Draw a picture of the location of the bubbles in the aquarium.

How Come, Huh?

Tuff is like hot, gooey oatmeal being thrown up into the air. When it comes down and lands on the table, it sticks together and forms layers of oatmeal gloop. Compare that to throwing dry oatmeal up into the air and having it come down as individual flakes, which is more like volcanic ash deposits that have had time to cool in the air and then fall to the Earth, remaining as loose, individual particles.

Dry Ice Ash Flows

Rock Profile: Tuff

How Was It Formed?

In addition to large eruptions that remove entire mountaintops and relocate them to various other areas, andesitic volcanos often produce smaller eruptions that emit hot gases and ash. In these gas and ash eruptions, the gases, which are heavier than air, spill out of the vent and over the side of the volcano. Think of it as a wave. The ash

then rides this wave of gas down the side of the volcano. If the ash is still hot and sticky when it erupts from the volcanic vent, it fuses together when it reaches the base of the volcano, forming a soft rock called **tuff** or **welded ash**.

What's It Used For?

Tuff is used for road base and landfill for construction projects. It is also an excellent stone for building construction. The warm colors and porosity (large number of holes) make it both attractive and a good insulator. If you look closely at a tuff sample or put it under a microscope, you will see long, dark crystals trapped among smaller gray and pink particles. This explains why tuff is called a **porphyritic** rock, or a mixture of large and small mineral grains.

Science Fair Extensions

42.   Use the idea of dry and wet oatmeal to create a model showing how tuff and volcanic ash pile up and create different kinds of igneous rocks.

43.   When these rocks are exposed to the elements, they weather and break down, and their minerals and nutrients are released into the soil. This is the reason that volcanic soils are among the richest and most productive in the world. Grind up some tuff and add it to potting soil to see if it makes a difference in plant growth.

Test Tube Ash Storm

Geologically Speaking ...

Quite often, when a volcano erupts, it produces lots of ash. The ash shoots up into the air and comes down around the base of the volcano. If the ash is dry, it produces a loose, powdery layer; if it is still sticky and hot, it will come down and "weld," or stick, together.

Occasionally, the ash contains minerals as well as very fine fragments of rock, and they all come together to form a beautiful and interesting rock that we call crystallized oatmeal mix.

This lab will give you an idea of how large the crystals are that could form and then float down through the air to form a rock that has large fragments and pieces of crystals in it.

Materials

1   20 mm x 150 mm test tube
1   1 oz. bottle of 10% potassium sulfate solution
1   1 oz. bottle of 70% isopropyl alcohol
1   1 mL pipette
1   Pencil
1   Sample of volcanic ash

Procedure

1.   Fill the test tube about two-thirds of the way with 10% potassium sulfate solution.

Test Tube Ash Storm

2. Open the bottle of isopropyl alcohol, squeeze the bulb of the pipette, and fill it by releasing the bulb. Slowly add 10 drops of alcohol to the test tube that has the potassium sulfate in it. You will immediately notice that a cloudy layer appears at the top of the tube. These are crystals starting to form.

ALCOHOL

POTASSIUM SULFATE
SOLUTION

TEST
TUBE

3. Add a couple more drops of isopropyl alcohol to increase the storm. Look closely and examine the crystals as they start to fall toward the bottom of the tube.

4. You will notice that, as the reaction proceeds, the crystals get larger and larger until they fall toward the bottom of the tube. Once the reaction starts, some of the smaller crystals also start to fall.

5. The entire reaction takes about five minutes to complete, so hang in there and be sure that you take time to observe everything. You can pour everything down the drain when you are finished. Then rinse out your tube.

Data & Observations

On a separate sheet of paper, draw a picture of the ash storm at full strength.

How Come, Huh?

This lab gives you an opportunity to observe crystals forming during a reaction. The potassium sulfate crystals precipitate out of solution when they come in contact with the alcohol. When a volcano erupts, it shoots a cloud of hot gases, dust, and minerals into the air.

This reaction is a metaphor for the reactions that may take place in that cloud of dust that shoots up into the air. Crystals may have time to form and, when they do, they become heavy enough to fall to the ground. If they are still wet and gooey, they glob together and form a rock similar to your piece of crystallized oatmeal mix.

Rock Profile: Volcanic Ash

How Was It Formed?

During violent rhyolitic eruptions, sometimes the mixture of magma, water, and trapped gas explodes so violently that the magma is shot into the air as tiny particles of molten lava. These particles cool very quickly and, because of their light nature, float to the ground as ash.

Science Fair Extensions

44. Volcanic ash is very rich in minerals and nutrients that are used by plants. If you happen to live out west where volcanos are abundant, gather up a pile of volcanic ash and use it in an experiment to see if its addition to the soil influences plant growth.

Big Idea 6

Intrusive igneous rocks are formed when molten rock, called magma, cools and solidifies slowly under the Earth's surface.

The Original Lava Lamp

Geologically Speaking ...

This will give you an idea of how huge bubbles and blobs of hot magma (also called plutons) rise through the overlying rock layers. Most of us have not seen many rocks float, let alone float through other rocks. That is exactly what they do, however, and it is due to differences in the densities of the materials. Pretend you jumped into your neighbor's transmogrifier and it shrunk you down to the size where you could see the atoms (particles) of a compound, which had become as big as marbles. If these marbles were all packed together as tightly as possible in a sack, you would see a very dense material. Everything is crammed together. If the sack were opened and the marbles were dumped onto the floor and spread out all over the place, then the material is not very dense. When lava heats up, the particles or atoms spread out, becoming less dense than the rock around them, which is made up of particles that are cooler and packed closer together. The cooler, surrounding rock actually pushes the less dense magma up toward the surface of the Earth.

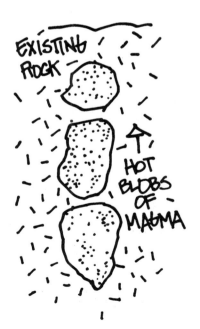

Materials

2   2-liter bottles, empty
1   Bottle of red food coloring
1   Tornado Tube
1   Kitchen sink (or plastic tub)
    Hot water
    Cold water
1   Sample of quartz monzonite

The Original Lava Lamp

Procedure

1. Fill one of the bottles with very hot water. Be careful not to burn yourself! Add several drops of red food coloring (any color will do, but we just happen to be fond of red). Replace the cap, and tip the bottle back and forth, mixing the food coloring into the water. When you have a nice dark color, you can move on to the next step. If your water color looks somewhat pale, add a couple more drops of food coloring and shake again.

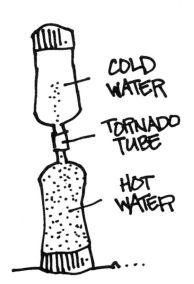

COLD WATER

TORNADO TUBE

HOT WATER

2. Remove the cap and screw the Tornado Tube connector onto the top of the bottle. Set this bottle in the sink or in the plastic tub.

3. Fill the second bottle with very cold water. No food coloring this time. Hold your hand over the opening, tip the bottle upside down, quickly place it in the Tornado Tube connector, and screw it into place.

4. Place the two bottles where you can observe the movement of the red water. The bottle of red, hot water should be on the bottom, with the cold water on top. The resulting movement of the water is due to the less dense hot water rising to the top and the more dense cold water dropping to the bottom, which results in a convection current in the water. Magma under the Earth's crust behaves in a similar way. The hottest magma rises through and above other magma that is not as hot.

Data & Observations

In the boxes below, draw pictures of your lava lamp after one minute and after five minutes.

How Come, Huh?

Forces under the Earth push hot magma up toward the surface of the Earth. Sometimes, this action causes the Earth to bow or bend upward. Other times, the lava fills cracks and crevices, or it melts the overlying layer and a large blob of magma oozes up into the rock layers and cools slowly over time.

The Original Lava Lamp

Rock Profile: Quartz Monzonite

How Was It Formed?

Quartz monzonite is formed when two tectonic plates collide into each other and rock melts under intense heat and pressure. Quartz monzonite looks similar to granite. Both quartz monzonite and granite are composed of essentially the same minerals, but in different proportions. When you get out into the field and are examining specimens that you collect, a magnifying lens and bright light will help to pick out the distinctions listed below:

Quartz	gray, irregular, glassy pieces
Plagioclase Feldspar	milky-white to tan, shiny, flat pieces
Alkali Feldspar	pink, shiny, flat pieces
Biotite Mica	black, shiny, flat pieces
Hornblende	black, shiny, flat pieces

What's It Used For?

Because its composition is similar to that of granite, quartz monzonite is also used as a building stone. The Mormon temple in downtown Salt Lake City, Utah is constructed almost entirely of quartz monzonite, which was hand-quarried in Little Cottonwood Canyon and then transported 15 miles by horse to the building site. Like granite, quartz monzonite is the host rock for lots of valuable ores, such as gold and silver. Miners and geologists look for these rocks as a clue to potential ore deposits in the vicinity.

A more contemporary use for this rock is by rock climbers who prize quartz monzonite exposures not only because they are composed of very hard rock but also because numerous, natural pathways are produced in the cooling process. These two conditions make for an ideal climbing opportunity.

Where Can I Find It?

Quartz monzonite is very common in central parts of the Appalachian Mountains, along the Wasatch Mountains of Utah (in particular, Little Cottonwood Canyon), and in the Sierra Nevada Mountains of Northern California. The most famous site is Yosemite, which is famous for a landform called Half Dome, which is made of quartz monzonite and can be seen from the Yosemite Valley. There are also several intrusions in Southern California; the best-known of these is Joshua Tree National Monument.

Science Fair Extensions

45. Compare the movement of the liquid layers in this experiment with the movement of liquids in "lava lamps" that are available commercially. Do some reading and determine how the movement of these liquids is similar to and different from the real blobs under the Earth's surface.

Igneous Fudge

Geologically Speaking ...

This lab will help you understand how the cooling rate of lava influences the size of the crystals found in the rock that is produced. The crystal size classifies the rock as either intrusive or extrusive igneous. We are going to use my mom's prize-winning fudge recipe and cool one half of the batch slowly and the other half quickly so we can compare the rate and size of crystal formation.

Materials

1   3 qt. sauce pan
1   Candy thermometer
1   Large wooden spoon
1   Pastry brush
2   9 inch x 9 inch pans, (size can vary somewhat)
1   Stove
1   Refrigerator
    and
    4 oz. semi-sweet chocolate
    3 1/2 cups sugar
1   Can of warm, homogenized milk
4   Tablespoons of light corn syrup
    1/4 cup of butter
2   Teaspoons of vanilla
    1/2 cup of walnuts or pecans (Texas version)
1   Sample of granite

Procedure

1. With adult supervision, place the pan on the stove and melt the semi-sweet chocolate over a very low flame.

2. Keeping the heat on low, gradually add the sugar, alternating with the warm milk. Continue to stir with the wooden spoon until the mixture is smooth.

3.   Increase the heat on the stove to medium and add the corn syrup, stirring continuously until the mixture starts to boil.

4.   Using the pastry brush and a little bit of water, rinse down the side of the pan and the spoon. Add the candy thermometer and continue cooking the fudge without stirring, if possible, until the temperature of the candy reaches 236°F.

5.   Remove the pan from the burner and let the mixture cool until it reaches 150°F. Add the vanilla and the butter, beating the fudge with the wooden spoon until the mixture dulls slightly. Mix the nuts into the fudge with the spoon.

6.   Pour half of the mixture into one pan and the other half of the mixture into the other pan. Leave the first pan of fudge on the counter at room temperature. Place the second pan in the refrigerator. Let both mixtures cool until hard. Cut the fudge from both pans in half and compare the texture of each sample. The fudge that cooled slowly should be grainy and have large sugar crystals. The fudge that cooled quickly should be smooth, show little in the way of crystals, and this will actually be the more desirable one to eat.

Igneous Fudge

Data & Observations

Draw a picture of each cross-section of fudge and describe the texture of each sample.

Refrigerator Fudge   Countertop Fudge

_____   _____
_____   _____
_____   _____
_____   _____
_____   _____

How Come, Huh?

As you now know, forces under the Earth push hot magma up toward the surface of the Earth. Sometimes, this action causes the Earth to bow or bend upward. Other times, the lava fills cracks and crevices, or it melts the overlying layer and a large blob of magma oozes up into the rock layers and cools slowly over time.

Rock Profile: Granite

How Was It Formed?

Granite often forms in mountainous areas that are produced by the collision of tectonic plates. The magma, formed from partially-melted rocks, rises and cools, and the minerals start to crystallize. Different minerals have different melting and "freezing" temperatures. Granite is composed of minerals that melt first and "freeze" last. These are quartz and alkali feldspar. As the hot magma rises toward the surface, it cools  slowly, giving the minerals in the magma time to find one another and form crystals that grow quite large. Evidence of this can be seen by looking at the size of the crystals in your specimen, especially compared to the fine-grained crystals found in the andesite specimen. The main difference between granite and quartz monzonite is that granite has more alkai feldspar, and quartz monzonite has more plagioclase feldspar.

If this hot, gooey magma cools and solidifies before reaching the surface, the rock is identified as granite. If this same mass of magma erupts onto the surface of the Earth to become an extrusive rock, it is classified as rhyolite. However, if it cools underground, erosion of the overlying material will eventually bring the granite to the surface where we can see it.

What's It Used For?

Granite is used extensively in building materials, monuments, and interior decoration. Like quartz monzonite, valuable ore deposits of gold and silver are often associated with granite deposits. When a glob of hot granitic magma takes a very long time to cool, it can lead to the creation of rocks called pegmatites. Pegmatites are very coarse-grained rocks with crystals than can be several meters long. These are quarried and sold to collectors and museums.

Igneous Fudge

Where Can I Find It?

Granite is very common in older rock formations on the east and west coasts of North America and in interior mountain areas like the Rocky Mountains. It is also common in the mountains of San Diego County, where some of the best samples of pegmatites also yield large, beautiful crystals that are commercially viable as precious gems.

Science Fair Extensions

46.   Temperature and crystal size are always related to each other. There are several crystal-growing experiments in the first part of this book. Take one of the recipes and design an experiment that is temperature-sensitive. Show how the size of the crystals that are grown is affected by the environment they are grown in.

47.   Collect several samples of granite and show the difference in crystal size, which, in turn, infers the amount of time the crystals have to grow. If possible, collect specimens from the top, center, and bottom of an exposed pluton, and try to determine from the crystal sizes which part of the pluton cooled first. It is not always where you would think it might be.

48.   Find a candy maker or chocolatier and ask if there are any other candy recipes that demonstrate this concept. With the help of an adult, try the recipes and have fun eating your experiments.

Globs of Gabbro

Geologically Speaking ...

This lab will help you to understand how the cooling rate of lava influences the size of its crystals.

Materials

1   1 oz. bottle of guar gum
1   1 oz. bottle of sodium tetraborate
1   Craft stick
1   5 oz. wax cup
1   1 mL pipette
1   Resealable baggie
1   Sample of gabbro
    Water

Procedure

1.   Take the cap off the bottle of guar gum. You will notice that this is a fine, white powder. Fill the cap half-full with this powder, and empty the powder into the wax cup. Put the cap back on the bottle to prevent spills.

2.   Add 3 ounces of water, just a little more than half the cup, to the powder. Stir the water and powder together with the craft stick. Keep in mind that this is basic chemistry, so if you use a little more or don't have quite enough, the experiment will probably still work. There are exceptions, though.

As you stir, you will notice that the solution starts to look like a thick pudding or yogurt. When you have reached that consistency, it is time to add another chemical.

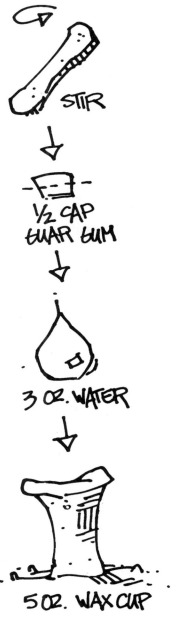

STIR

½ CAP GUAR GUM

3 OZ. WATER

5 OZ. WAX CUP

Globs of Gabbro

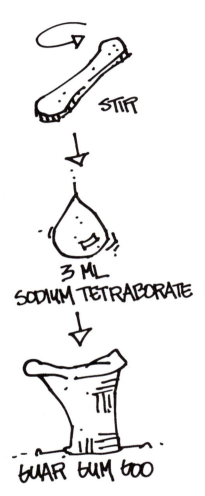

STIR

3 ML
SODIUM TETRABORATE

GUAR GUM GOO

3. Add 3 milliliters of the liquid sodium tetraborate and keep stirring. A gooey polymer will start to form immediately. The more you stir, the more cross-links you are forming between the long polymers. It takes a little time, but you will notice that the solution gets more rubbery. When it gets to a nice rubbery to solid consistency, empty it out into your hand and play with it.

4. To understand more of how gabbro oozes up into the layers of the Earth's crust, take the rubbery blob in your hand and place your other hand over the top.

Spreading your fingers out a bit, gently squeeze the gummy blob so that it starts to slowly ooze through your fingertips and up onto the top of your hand.

5. Get the glob back in a single pile in the palm of your hand and place your second hand around the glob so that there is an opening up through the center of the palm of your hand. Gently squeeze the glob and watch as the guar gum oozes up through the center. This is kind of how gabbro fills a lava tube near the surface of the Earth.

6. When you are all done, put the mess back into the cup, put it in a resealable baggie, and take it home.

Data & Observations

Draw a picture of how each blob might ooze up and form new globs of magma.

How Come, Huh?

If you could see a large section of this rock on the side of a volcano, you would see folds, bubbles, and movement. It is much harder in a small section, but you should get an idea of how this rock came to be formed.

Globs of Gabbro

Rock Profile: Gabbro

How Was It Formed?

Gabbro is the most common form
of magma. This magma, formed from
partially-melted rocks, rises and cools,
and the minerals start to crystallize. Different minerals have different melting
and "freezing" temperatures. Gabbro is
composed of minerals that melt last and
"freeze" first. As the hot magma rises toward the surface, it cools
slowly, giving the minerals in the magma time to find one another and
form crystals that grow quite large. The main difference between
gabbro and quartz monzonite and granite is that it has more of the
darker minerals.

If this hot, gooey magma cools and solidifies before reaching
the surface, the rock is identified as basalt. However, if it cools
underground, erosion of the overlying material will eventually bring
the gabbro to the surface where we can see it.

What's It Used For?

Gabbro is used extensively in building materials and road base.
It is not very attractive, so it is used for backfill, highway construction,
and other commerical uses.

Where Can I Find It?

Gabbro is very common. It is associated with large deposits of
basalt. It can be found in Southern Idaho, throughout Oregon and
Washington, in portions of Northern California, and occasionally in
Arizona, New Mexico, and the corner of West Texas.

Science Fair Extensions

49. Compare the general colors of quartz monzonite, gabbro,
and granite. List the individual minerals found in each specimen and
determine if they influence the overall color of the specimen.

Igneous Rock Review

Geologically Speaking ...

Igneous rocks are produced when hot, molten rock hardens. There are two kinds of igneous rocks:

A. Intrusive (in • true • sive) Igneous Rocks. This group is produced when molten rock, called magma, cools _inside_ the crust below the surface of the Earth. The magma remains *in*side in the *in*terior of the Earth. Intrusive rocks form when a huge glob of magma penetrates upward from the mantle into the crust of the Earth, forming what is called an *igneous intrusion*. This hot mass of molten rock slowly cools over hundreds or thousands of years until it becomes a solid rock formation called a *pluton*. Plutons are eventually exposed on the surface by a combination of mountain-building and erosion processes.

B. Extrusive (ex • true • sive) Igneous Rocks. This group is produced when the same molten rock, or magma, finds its way to the _outside_ of the Earth's crust. Once outside the crust, where it is called lava, it cools quickly. The only difference between the intrusive magma and the extrusive lava is that the magma was successful in pushing all the way to the surface of the Earth. The magma *ex*its, or more poetically, *ex*cuses itself from the proverbial bowels of the Earth and cools quickly out in the fresh air and sunshine. One way that this happens is that volcanos erupt and *ex*pel molten lava, sometimes ash, and possibly a fair amount of hot gas to produce a number of extrusive igneous rocks. These include pumice, scoria, andesite, and obsidian. There are also cracks in the crust of the Earth that open up and ooze lava over hundreds of square miles of ground. These are called *basalt flood plains* and are found all over the Pacific Northwest.

Materials

1   Piece of quartz monzonite
1   Piece of andesite
1   Piece of red lava cinder
1   Hand lens
1   Pencil

Igneous Rock Review

Procedure

1. First, examine all three of the igneous rocks in your collection with your hand lens. The quartz monzonite is the black, white, and gray speckled rock; the andesite is a blue-gray color with some small speckles; the red lava cinder should stick out like a sore thumb.

2. Draw a picture of each rock on a separate sheet of paper. Be sure to label your drawings.

3. As you examined your rock samples, you should have looked for spots of different color, different sheen, and different fracture patterns. Each of these spots on the rock is what geologists call a **grain**. These grains are most often a single mineral crystal. You probably noticed that, in some samples, the grains were large and very obvious, and in others, you were not able to see the grains at all.

4. There are two BIG IDEAS that you will take away from this activity:
   A) Big grains take a longer time to grow than little grains.
   B) Molten rocks take longer to cool underground than above ground.
   Using these BIG IDEAS, you can tell whether a particular sample cooled underground slowly (these are the intrusive igneous rocks) or cooled quickly on the surface (these are the extrusive igneous rocks).

5. However, you are not off the hook that easily. What about a rock sample that has both big *and* tiny crystals? Is it possible for molten rock to cool both below *and* on the surface of the Earth? Inquiring minds want to know. Think about this for a moment, then keep going. For purposes of a classroom discussion: Is it absolutely necessary for molten rock to stay in one place the whole time it cools? Keep thinking.

Dig It! • *Lockwood DeWitt & B. K. Hixson*

6.   If you guessed that the rocks with both fine and coarse grains in the same sample were formed by cooling for a while underground first and then erupting out onto the surface, you got it right. This texture is called **porphyritic (poor • fur • it • ick)**. It's quite common in areas where there are lots of volcanos, especially volcanos that produce andesite. The lava fills the vent, or neck, of the volcano and sits there for a while, cooling and forming large, visible mineral grains. Then boom! The volcano explodes, the lava oozes out onto the ground, and it cools so fast that the rest of the grains are too small to see with the naked eye. It's kind of like a chocolate chip cookie. The chips are the large mineral grains that cooled slowly, and the rest of the cookie is made of the smaller grains that cooled rapidly.

Data & Observations

Sort your rocks into 3 groups: those that cooled underground in hot, sealed chambers (intrusive); those that came above ground as a fiery flow of lava (extrusive); and those that escaped their chambers after a period of time to reach the surface (porphyritic).

Rock Name	Description	Type
Quartz Monzonite		
Andesite		
Red Lava Cinder		

Igneous Rock Review

Now that you have been introduced to extrusive and intrusive igneous rocks, take a minute to review and regroup before moving on to the sedimentary rock group. We have filled in the table on the next page with information that, based on your study of individual specimens and completion of the experiments, should start to make some sense to you. If you look at the granitic rocks, you'll see that they are made up of light-colored minerals that melt at lower temperatures. The light-colored minerals would then naturally give most of the rocks in this group a lighter color. Because they are high in silica content, they would be sticky, meaning that they would not flow very well. It also would be more likely that a lot of pressure would build up and the volcanos would explode, producing pyroclastic material. On the other hand, the basaltic rocks are made primarily out of dark-colored minerals that melt at higher temperatures. The darker minerals would produce a darker-colored rock, which is why basalt and scoria are commonly found as black specimens. They don't have as much silica, so they are runny and flow easily. This is why large areas of land are covered with basalt floods. You are less likely to find pyroclastic materials in these areas. Review the information until you have a clear understanding of the igneous types and then head off to the sedimentary rock pages.

Silica Content	High (above 66%)	Medium (52-66%)	Low (45-51%)
Extrusive Igneous Rock	Obsidian Pumice	Andesite Basalt	Red Cinders Rhyolite
Intrusive Igneous Rock	Granite	Quartz Monzonite	Gabbro
Viscosity (Gooeyness)	Thick Sticky	Intermediate	Fluid Runny
Tendency to Produce Flows	Low	Intermediate	High
Tendency to Produce Pyroclasts	High	Intermediate	Low
Minerals	Quartz Orthoclase Na Plagioclase	Amphibole Biotite Plagioclase	Magnetite Ca Plagioclase Pyroxene Olivine
Color (Usually)	Light	Intermediate	Dark
Melting Point	Lowest 700-800 °C	Intermediate 1100-1200 °C	Highest 1300-1500 °C

Big Idea 7

Organic sedimentary rocks are formed when living matter dies, piles up, and is compressed into rock.

Macaroni Coquina

Geologically Speaking ...

Coquina is formed near ocean shorelines in areas that have large populations of shelled animals like clams, oysters, snails, and horn corals, as well as a relatively low amounts of sediment coming from the land. When a crustacean dies, the wave action will usually pulverize its shell into fragments. The smallest pieces, the size of small sand or mud particles, are washed away to deeper, calmer waters, where they settle. The coarse fragments, the size of larger sand grains or pebbles, are more difficult to wash away. These accumulate to form the equivalent of a beach. As this "shell beach" sits, minerals from the ocean water gently cement the fragments together to form solid rock. This cementing is not very strong, however, so coquina is normally picked apart very easily.

This lab will allow you to make a sample of coquina using different kinds of macaroni that is cemented together using glue. The macaroni obviously represents the shells of the marine animals, and the glue is the mineral matter that holds them together.

Materials

1   5 oz. wax cup
    White glue (2 tbsp.)
1   Macaroni, 1/2 cup
        assorted shapes and sizes
1   Craft stick
1   Pie tin
    Water
1   Sample of coquina

Macaroni Coquina

WHITE GLUE

↓

WATER

↓

MACARONI

↓

5 OZ. WAX CUP

Procedure

1. Using the heel of your thumb, crush some of the macaroni. This mimics the way wave activity breaks up shells at the shoreline. We don't want everything crushed. We just want some fragments mixed in with the whole pieces.

2. Pour the macaroni into the wax cup, add an ounce of water, and stir with the craft stick until the macaroni is wet. Pour off the excess water.

3. Drizzle the glue over the wet macaroni. Stir with the craft stick to distribute the glue evenly.

4. Empty the whole mess into the pie tin and place it in an area to dry where younger siblings and pets won't eat it.

5. After the material has dried thoroughly (overnight to a day), remove it from the tin and show it to your friends and neighbors.

6. Record your observations in the spaces provided on the next page.

Data & Observations

In the spaces that are provided below, draw a picture of your coquina sample as well as the macaroni coquina sample that you created. Note the similarities and differences.

Similarities: _____

_____

_____

Differences: _____

_____

_____

How Come, Huh?

In this lab, we made an artificial coquina by mixing artificial shells (macaroni) after breaking them up a little. This is the same way waves at the shore mix and break real shells. We used water and white glue to cement everything together into a coherent mass (a rock). In the real world, water dissolves a little of the calcite from the shells, and some of that calcite precipitates back out and cements the shells together into a coherent rock. Incidentally, calcite is most often white or colorless, so white glue is a good substitute.

Macaroni Coquina

Rock Profile: Coquina

How Was It Formed?

Coquina forms easily and quickly under the right conditions, and has been forming in the same areas along the coast for countless years. Older coquina can sometimes be found in limestone beds and tends to be more completely cemented. Aside from shells, coquina often has fragments of  hard parts from less familiar organisms, such as sponge spicules (small needle-like spikes), bryozoans, fragments of coral, and skeletons or "tests" from single-celled animals.

More trivia: Coquina is found in great abundance on the Florida Coast, an area explored thoroughly by the Spanish years ago. The Spanish word for shell is "concha." "Coquina" means, literally, "little shells." Clever folks, those Conquistadors.

What's It Used For?

Coquina is one type of limestone. It is occasionally used as an architectural and decorative stone, and has been sold as decorative coasters for drinks. In areas where it is abundant, coquina is often crushed and used in concrete or as fill for gravel roads, instead of the usual sand and gravel.

Science Fair Extensions

50. Take a peek at the individual shells found in your specimen of coquina and, using a guide, determine their names. If you have an extensive guide to your area, you can also determine if your coquina specimen is a near-shore or off-shore specimen.

51. Using your coquina specimen as a guide, recreate an actual marine environment using three-dimensional paper models of your marine animals. Try to recreate the correct proportion of animals in the sample as well as their correct sizes.

Distilled Fossils

Geologically Speaking ...

Coal is an extremely important commodity. It is not only a source of heat and energy, but it also allows us to produce plastics, pesticides, medicines, lubricants, and a host of other goods. Of all the fossil energy sources currently used in North America, coal is the most likely to last for the long term—several centuries by some estimates.

Because of the various uses that we have for coal, it will be an economically important geological resource for generations to come. You are going to heat a small piece of coal and observe firsthand a couple of its by-products.

Materials

1 Small chip of bituminous coal
   (the size of a pea)
1 Pyrex test tube
1 Test tube holder
1 Propane torch
1 Disposable pie tin
1 Pair of goggles
1 Sample of bituminous coal
1 Sample of anthracite coal
1 Sample of lignite coal

Procedure

1. Goggles on and adult supervision! Place the coal chip in the test tube, and pick up the tube with the holder. Hold the bottom of the tube over the heat source for a few minutes.

Distilled Fossils

Technique Time: Hold the tube just over the top of the flame, rather than in the flame. This region is the hottest part of the flame and will not deposit soot on the outside of the tube. Hold the test tube at an angle, so the mouth is not over the flame. The gas that is produced is flammable and, even though the quantity generated is small, it is startling to have a second flame pop up. Holding the test tube at an angle will also keep the walls of the tube cooler, which will aid in the collecting of the liquid portion and will also keep the clamp from overheating.

2.   As the piece of coal heats, you will notice a thick, oily odor caused by heating the coal. Also pay attention to the piece of coal. You may be able to see vapor and liquid bubbling from the fragment. The escaping gas is called **coal gas**, and was used during the 1800s to light street lamps and lamps in city houses.

3.   The brown, oily material on the test tube walls is **coal tar**. Coal tar contains different substances that can be separated for use in the chemical industry. It is used in the production of many organic compounds, including dyes, plastic and synthetic textiles, pesticides, medicines, and much more. Researchers are also looking for ways to use it as a petroleum (oil) substitute.

4. The solid left over on the bottom of the tube is called **coke** (not to be confused with the soda pop of the same name). Heating bituminous coal drives off compounds, called volatile compounds, that vaporize easily and leave behind a purer form of carbon. Because of its greater purity, it releases more heat when burned than "raw" coal of similar weight. Metallurgy, the purifying and shaping of metal, still uses a great deal of coke.

Data & Observations

Draw a picture of the coal being heated, and label and identify the following: *coal gas*, *coal tar*, and *coke*. Then list the possible uses of each by-product.

Distilled Fossils

How Come, Huh?

Throughout millions of years of Earth's history, the interiors of continents have occasionally been covered by warm, shallow seas. During these periods, vast areas were covered by swamps, much like today's Everglades or the bayous of the lower Mississippi. Shrubs, ferns, and various types of trees covered hundreds of square miles. When these plants died, they fell into the water but decayed only partially. Warm, stagnant water does not hold oxygen very well, but plant tissue needs oxygen in order to rot completely. As a result, layers and layers of plant material accumulated in the water much faster than the material could decay. This went on over millions of years, resulting in the piling up of literally tons and tons of dead plant matter.

As the plates of the Earth continued to move, changes in sea levels resulted in the burial of these layers under thick sediment. As the amount of sediment increased, the pressure and temperature also increased, cooking the plant matter slowly to form coal. By the way, if you find this recipe in your family cookbook, be assured that it is very old. Anyway, during this final step, water and gases were squished out along with the mud and sand, leaving nearly pure carbon.

Rock Profile: Coal

How Was It Formed?

True coal comes in two forms, **bituminous** and **anthracite**. Anthracite is simply bituminous coal that has been exposed to greater heat and pressure and is found in areas that have been subjected to intense mountain-building forces. This kind of coal is purer in quality and burns hotter. Bituminous coal is by far the more abundant. It is easy to identify because of its clearly layered appearance and because it is easy to split. Peat is simply plant material that has accumulated in a bog or swamp and has barely changed from its original form. Lignite has undergone somewhat more compaction, and can be thought of as a substance that is halfway between coal and peat.

What's It Used For?

Coal is used to generate electricity, and is also heated to form various materials, such as coal tar, which is used widely in the chemical industry. Nearly all dyes and even medicines, such as aspirin, come indirectly from coal.

Coal has also contributed to the naming of at least one species of dog. A "collier" is a person who works with or sells coal, and a "collie" is a dog. For those people familiar with dogs, they may know that border collies are almost completely black, just like colliers are after a hard day's work.

Where Can I Find It?

Coal can be found in the upper Midwest (Ohio, West Virginia, Pennsylvania, Kentucky, Illinois, Indiana, and Tennessee) and in the central Rocky Mountain states (Utah, Colorado, Montana, and Wyoming).

Science Fair Extensions

52. Determine the heat value of different kinds of coal. If you have access to a bomb calorimeter, using it would be one way to calculate the amount of heat energy stored. If one is not available, there are a couple of other ways available to folks who stick their noses into books and do some research.

Big Idea 8

Chemical sedimentary rocks are formed when minerals dissolved in water crystallize out, or precipitate, from solution.

Dig It! • Lockwood DeWitt & B. K. Hixson

Instant Salt Flats

Geologically Speaking ...

Gypsum is an **evaporite** mineral, formed when water evaporates and leaves behind a layer of dissolved minerals. Beds of gypsum are present almost everywhere halite (salt) is present, and it is generally believed to have been deposited as a result of bays which had restricted circulation from the ocean and high evaporation rates.

Gypsum is commonly deposited in desert areas today, particularly in enclosed basins (valleys completely surrounded by mountains with no outlets for water) that lose all of their incoming water through evaporation. It will often form thin seams in sediments deposited under dry conditions, and crystal clusters, called desert roses, which grow as water wicks up through the soil, carrying dissolved minerals. This lab will show you how dissolved minerals can be deposited by evaporation.

Materials

1   Glass or ceramic dish <u>or</u> *disposable* metal pan
    (Salt will corrode metal; do not use good metal kitchenware.)
1   Cup of hot water
1   Spoon
    Salt, 1/2 c.
5   Pennies
1   Tbsp. soil
1   Tbsp. baking soda
1   Sample of halite
1   Sample of gypsum

Procedure

1. Slowly pour the salt into the cup of hot water, stirring it with the spoon until it dissolves. Let it sit for a few minutes, then stir again.

Instant Salt Flats

SALT

HOT WATER

CUP

2.   Let the salt water sit for another minute to settle. Then pour it into the pan.

3.   Place the pan in an open area until all of the water has evaporated.   As the water evaporates, it leaves the dissolved salt behind, forming the crystals you see. Depending on the conditions, you may have nice, large crystals or many small, granular crystals.

4.   Record your observations over a period of time. Note the crystals' size, abundance, and distribution. Compare the samples of halite and gypsum to the minerals that are deposited around the perimeter of your dish.

5.   When the lab is complete, you can toss everything into the sink, rinse it out, and put the dish and other items away.

How Come, Huh?

Nearly all halite, or rock salt, was formed when a body of salt water evaporated. When the water left the solution, the salt and other minerals that were dissolved in the water remained. These types of deposits are believed to have been created when portions of ancient oceans formed that did not have much fresh water flowing into them and, at the time, had poor circulation with the rest of the oceans. In these conditions, as the flow of water from the ocean to that area continued, the concentration of salt in the water steadily increased until it became saturated and started to crystallize out of solution.

Rock Profile: Halite

How Was It Formed?

Enclosed basins in desert areas are another environment for halite and similar minerals. Normally, snow or rain that falls on mountain ranges or plains flows to the ocean, but in mountainous areas like Nevada and Utah, where rainfall is low and basins have formed that have no outlet to the ocean, the water gets  trapped. Under wet (high or normal) conditions, water will dissolve salt from the surrounding rock, carry it to the valley floor, and then evaporate. When the water evaporates, the salt is left behind.

What's It Used For?

Halite is used in flavoring foods, food processing, food preservation, and de-icing roads and sidewalks in the wintertime. It is also important in the chemical industry as a basic source of both sodium and chlorine. Hydrochloric acid is manufactured from halite.

Where Can I Find It?

Halite can be found in the arid basins of the western U.S., Death Valley National Monument in California, the Salton Sea in Southern California, and the Great Salt Lake area in Utah. Thick, buried beds of salt are found in the southern Great Lakes area, in the Gulf Coast, in the Great Plains of Kansas, and in Southern Canada.

Instant Salt Flats

Rock Profile: Gypsum

How Was It Formed?

Gypsum is an **evaporite (e • vap • oar
• ite)** mineral, formed when water evaporates
and leaves behind a layer of dissolved minerals. Beds of gypsum are present almost everywhere halite is present, and it is generally
believed to have been deposited as a result of
bays which had restricted circulation from the
ocean and which had high evaporation rates.

Like halite, gypsum is commonly de-
posited in desert areas today, particularly in enclosed basins (valleys
completely surrounded by mountains with no outlets for water) that lose
all of their incoming water through evaporation. For those of you keeping
score, gypsum is less soluble than halite, precipitates (comes out of
solution) more easily, and has more difficulty being carried away in
solution. Because of these properties, gypsum tends to form more easily
than halite and hangs around for longer periods of time on the Earth's
surface. It will often form thin seams in sediments deposited under dry
conditions, and crystal clusters, called desert roses, which grow as water
wicks up through the soil carrying dissolved minerals.

What's It Used For?

The application familiar to almost everyone is that gypsum is
used to make those obnoxious sticks of chalk that screech as you drag
them across the blackboard. It is also dehydrated, then powdered to form
Plaster of Paris. When water is added, the powder recrystallizes to
gypsum and hardens. It is used in construction as wallboard, for hobby
projects, and is still occasionally called into service to hold broken bones
in place.

Where Can I Find It?

Gypsum is fairly common in arid (dry) regions. It shows up in
bedded rocks and in deposits of windblown sands in White Sands, NM.

Science Fair Extensions

53. *Tilted Evaporites*

In many of the western salt basins, notably Death Valley, the salt deposits are much thicker on one side of the basin than the other. Repeat the Instant Salt Flats lab, but as the water evaporates, place pennies under one end of the dish, gradually stacking them higher and higher. If the water is evaporating quickly, you may need to do this every hour or two. If it's evaporating slowly, once or twice a day may be appropriate. Tilting the dish mimics the way that mountain-building activity slowly tilts basins in the west.

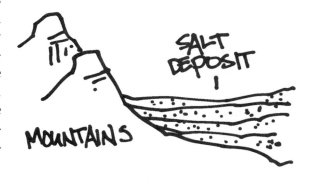

54. *Dirty Evaporites*

Repeat Instant Salt Flats, adding a tablespoon of soil and a tablespoon of baking soda. Let the water evaporate as before, and examine the new salt flat. This model is somewhat more realistic, and your deposit will probably look a little more like a real evaporite sample. In the real world, impurities, such as mud and other mineral salts, interfere with the growth of otherwise-pure crystals. Because of this, natural evaporite deposits often look dirty, and large crystals are rare. Other minerals found in evaporite deposits include sylvite, gypsum, anhydrite, calcite, aragonite, dolomite, epsomite, and a wide variety of borax minerals. Epsomite is the geological term for epsom salts.

Anhydrite is the mineral name for the material you know as Plaster of Paris, before water has been added, and gypsum is the name for the mineral formed when you add water to the plaster powder. Sylvite is frequently used as a salt substitute: It is potassium chloride instead of sodium chloride, and it can help lower blood sodium.

Instant Salt Flats

55. *Layered Evaporites*

Repeat Instant Salt Flats several times using the same salt dish, adding to the previous salt layers each time. If you do this enough times, you will create a layered salt bed. This is what is thought to occur in arid regions. The winter rains wash new mineral waters into the basins. Summer arrives, and with the heat, the evaporation of the water increases. This produces a new crop of crystals that cover up the salt deposits from the previous year. You may want to create a few "dirty" evaporite layers between the "clean" ones to show the layering more clearly.

SALT
SOLUTION

PIE TIN

COINS

Bottle Geyser

Geologically Speaking ...

This lab will simulate the action of a geyser. When the bottle is just sitting on a table, all the forces acting on it are equal. The pressure of the atmosphere inside the bottle is equal to the pressure outside the bottle. Everything is equal and kosher: You have the status quo, also known as equilibrium. When you start to force air into the bottle, the balance of forces is altered. This, of course, irritates the air particles being crammed inside the bottle. The particles of air smooshed into the bottle don't have as much room as they used to, so they push the water molecules up into the straw and out into the air where they proceed to dampen your once-dry table so they can spread out. When the air pressure is once again equal inside and out and everybody has enough space, the water stops being pushed from the bottle.

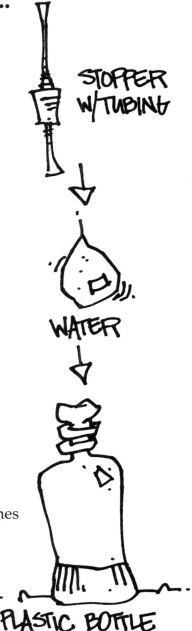

STOPPER W/TUBING

WATER

PLASTIC BOTTLE

Materials

1   Plastic bottle, 2 liter
1   #3, one-hole stopper, rubber
1   Length of glass tubing, 12 inches
1   Bottle of liquid soap
    Water
1   Sample of geyserite

Bottle Geyser

Procedure

1. Fill the bottle with water, leaving 2 inches of air at the top.

2. Holding it in one hand, dip the glass rod into the bottle of soap so that the end becomes gooey. Stick the soapy end of the glass rod into the hole in the stopper and carefully slide the glass tubing one-third of the way through the stopper. Use the illustration on the previous page as a guide for judging how far to slide the stopper.

3. Insert the stopper/glass tube apparatus into the neck of the bottle, leaving the tallest part of the glass tube sticking up. Refer to the illustration below.

4. Take a deep breath and blow into the glass tube until you can no longer force any air into the bottle. Observe what happens to the bubbles as they enter the bottle, and also pay attention to how the sides of the bottle feel.

5. When the bottle finally starts to win and you can't blow any more air into it, quickly remove your face. A stream of water should shoot up into the air (and if you're not fast enough, all over your face).

6. Once you get done laughing, repeat the experiment and, this time, have someone else, like your little sister, blow into the bottle while you make the observations. Not only is it fun to "share" this experiment, it also keeps you much drier.

Data & Observations

On the lines provided below, explain what you observed and why you think that the water shot into the air.

_____

_____

_____

_____

_____

How Come, Huh?

A geyser works the same way the materials in your experiment worked. Water in an underground chamber comes in contact with a layer of hot rock. The rock heats the water and starts to boil, forming steam in the process. The steam needs more room to move around because it is a gas, so the presence of the steam actually increases the pressure inside the rock chamber. When the pressure gets great enough, the water is shoved out of the ground. A geyser is born.

Bottle Geyser

Rock Profile: Geyserite

How Was It Formed?

The terms "geyser" and "geyserite" come from Geysir, Iceland, where these geological features were first studied and recognized as being distinct from hot springs.

Geyserite is formed when mineral-rich water boils from the ground, erupting into the air. Once the water is outside the ground, it immediately begins to cool and evaporate, depositing a thin layer of minerals near the geyser. This happens several times a day and, over time, these thin mineral layers add up to large layers of rock.

The process that allows this to happen starts underground. A layer of rock is near the Earth's surface. Water comes in contact with this hot rock and is heated. As the water sits underground, slowly heating up, it dissolves minerals from the rocks surrounding it. After a period of time, the water gets so hot that it starts to boil and erupt. When the hot water erupts to the surface, it cools very quickly and can no longer carry many dissolved minerals. These minerals are then deposited around the geyser.

What's It Used For?

Because it is relatively rare and is present only as small surface deposits where it is found, geyserite does not have much use beyond being a curiosity for collectors.

Where Can I Find It?

By definition, this kind of rock is found only around geysers, and geysers tend to be somewhat scarce. It is abundant in Yellowstone National Park, which contains more geysers than any other location on Earth. It can also be found at The Geysers, California, or at Crystal Geyser near Green River, Utah. This last geyser is actually a cold water geyser, propelled out of the ground by carbon dioxide.

Science Fair Extensions

56. Build a model of the geyser, Old Faithful, found in Yellowstone National Park. Create the model so that you can show a cross-section of the Earth's crust, the chamber where the water is heated, and the presence or location of the aquifer that feeds the chamber. Demonstrate the eruption by designing it in a mechanical squeeze bottle.

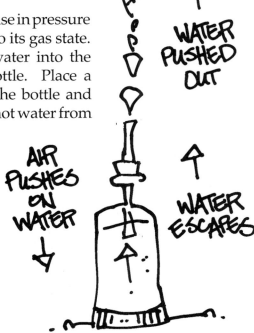

57. Demonstrate the increase in pressure that is created by heating water to its gas state. To do this, place 10 drops of water into the bottom of a thick, glass pop bottle. Place a rubber balloon over the top of the bottle and hold the bottle under a stream of hot water from your kitchen faucet. Observe what happens to the balloon and then explain how this same energy could erupt a geyser.

58. Do a little research and find a chemistry experiment that proves that as super saturated solutions cool, their ability to hold chemicals (minerals) in solution is reduced.

Making Limestone

Geologically Speaking ...

Limestone is an extremely common and important type of rock. This is a fun and interesting lab that shows one way limestone can form.

Materials

1   Lime, a.k.a. calcium oxide, 1 oz. (available from gardening stores)
2   Pop bottles, 2 liters each, rinsed
1   Funnel
2   Paper napkins or paper towels
1   Length rubber tubing or straw, 8 inches
1   Dropper
    Water
    Vinegar
1   Pair of goggles
1   Pair of rubber gloves

Procedure

NOTE: Lime is irritating to the eyes and to some people's skin. We recommend that goggles and rubber gloves be used anytime there is a chance that the lime water or lime dust could get onto you.

1.   Pour the lime into one of the bottles. Fill the bottle about 3/4-full of water, cap, and shake well. Let it sit for 10 minutes, then shake it again. Let it sit for half an hour to settle.

CALCIUM OXIDE

WATER

2 LITER BOTTLE

2. Fold a napkin into a cone shape and place it into the funnel. Wet it with tap water, and let the excess water drip off.

3. Place the funnel into the second bottle and carefully pour off the liquid from the first bottle. Try to avoid transferring the lime into the second bottle. You don't need all the liquid from the first bottle, so when the lime starts to get mixed up again, just leave the remaining liquid.

4. You should now have a nearly-clear liquid in the second bottle. This is called limewater; it's just water saturated with calcium oxide. Now for the fun part: Take the rubber tubing or straw and blow bubbles into the limewater. As you exhale through the limewater, you will see it get cloudy. The calcium oxide is reacting with carbon dioxide from your breath to form calcite, which precipitates as tiny crystals. This is a quick and easy test for carbon dioxide, but what we're interested in here is the precipitate.

5. Let's make sure that what we have is actually calcite. Make a second filter from a napkin or paper towel for your funnel and wet it as before. Put the funnel into a sink with the stem down the drain—we're going to dispose of the liquid part and save the cloudy precipitate.

This time, we want to get as much of the precipitate out as we can, so swirl the liquid and pour some into the funnel. A note on technique: If you fill the funnel up just a little, you'll end up concentrating the precipitate into the bottom of

Making Limestone

the filter, rather than having it spread all over the sides. This will make the next step easier.

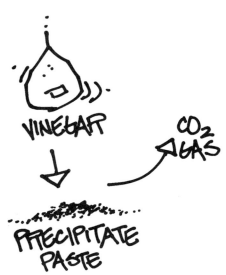

VINEGAR

CO_2 GAS

PRECIPITATE PASTE

6. After you've collected all the precipitate you can, let the filter drip dry for a few minutes, then pull the filter out and spread it open on a flat surface. You should be able to see a small pile of white goo down in the corner of the napkin/filter. This is the precipitate from the reaction of your breath with the limewater.

7. Using a dropper, deposit a couple of drops of vinegar onto the goo. You should see it fizz vigorously. This shows that the goo is probably calcite—just the same as the limey mud we talked about with respect to limestone. The material you made is exactly the same as a major component of many limestones. Another interesting thing to consider is that the bubbles from the fizzing are carbon dioxide—the very same molecules that you exhaled just a few minutes ago.

8. You can cap the first bottle with the lime in it and save it to do this experiment again some rainy day, or rinse it out and pour it down the drain.

How Come, Huh?

Limestone can form as a direct precipitate from warm marine water. Ocean water is very nearly saturated with respect to calcite, and mixing in a little more carbon dioxide can be just the thing to make calcite precipitate. Many marine organisms take advantage of this to make their shells, although the exact chemistry of how they make calcite crystallize is not well understood. But the basic idea of calcium oxide combining with carbon dioxide to form calcite is certainly at the core of making shells, even if we don't know the details.

Rock Profile: Limestone

How Was It Formed?

Limestone is an extremely com-mon and important type of rock. It is made up almost entirely of very small crystals of the mineral, calcite. If you've been working through this book from the beginning, you will remember that calcite fizzes when you drop an acid (vinegar, for example) onto it. So a quick and easy test for limestone is the fizz test.

The calcite that makes up a piece of limestone can come from several places. In warm, marine (ocean) water, calcite can precipitate directly from solution. This generally makes a fine-grained limey mud. Limey mud makes up the bulk of some limestone layers; it's most often a bland gray color, but it can have earthy (red, pink, orange, yellow, green) colors, and if there's a lot of organic material in the rock, it can be black like coal.

A second source of calcite is from shells of aquatic creatures. Limestone is an excellent rock for preserving fossils, and fossils in huge numbers may be present in even a small piece of limestone. Coquina, which we discussed a few pages back, is a special case of limestone where almost the entire rock is composed of shells and shell fragments. Corals, mollusks, brachiopods, and many other organisms have shells made of calcite.

Making Limestone

A third source of calcite is recrystallization. As the limey sediment and shells are compressed and water moves through, the calcite can dissolve from one place and precipitate in another place. This action helps cement the whole pile together, and frequently leaves patches of crystals that are visible to the eye or with a hand lens.

What's It Used For?

Limestone is used extensively as road gravel and in construction. When it is heated to drive off carbon dioxide, the remains are called lime. This is the key ingredient in cement. Lime is also used extensively as a soil conditioner, making soil less acid and more basic. Stomach acid is neutralized by calcite. We don't recommend that you go gnaw on a piece of limestone next time you have heartburn, but many over-the-counter remedies use purified calcite as their main ingredient. These same tablets are used as dietary calcium supplements.

Where Can I Find It?

Limestone is deposited mainly in warm, shallow marine environments, so it can be found forming in tropical oceans today. The interior of North America was covered by shallow ocean water frequently in the past, and the continent was closer to the equator. So the interior of the U.S., from the Appalachians to the Sierra Nevadas, has abundant beds of limestone.

Science Fair Extensions

59. Plunk a piece of limestone into a bottle of distilled vinegar and observe what happens over a period of time.

60. Take the same rock, grind it into a powder using a mortar and pestle, add vinegar, and observe the difference.

Big Idea 9

Clastic sedimentary rocks are formed from weathered and eroded pieces of previously existing rocks that got deposited together and smooshed and cemented into rock.

Conglomerate Stew

Geologically Speaking ...

The word "clastic" comes from a root meaning "fragment." So "clastic" rocks are made up of fragments of other rocks. Those other rocks might be igneous, metamorphic, or even other clastic sedimentary rocks. But the general idea is that older rocks sit on the Earth's surface and are broken down by weathering. These broken, weathered pieces are then transported, most often by running water but also by wind and ice, and piled up in a basin or in the nearest ocean. As more and more stuff piles up, pressure and precipitation cement the individual grains together, making a sedimentary rock. Incidentally (and logically, I guess), after it has been deposited but before it solidifies, the broken, weathered fragments are called sediment. This term is used whether the pieces are invisibly tiny, like clay, or huge, like boulders. It's all sediment.

However, this range of size is important for a couple of reasons. First, in terms of recognizing and naming the rock, the size of the sediment fragments determines what the rock is. You are probably familiar with mud, sand, and pebbles. That'll make these rocks easy to recognize: Mudstone is made of mud, sandstone is made of sand, and conglomerate is made of pebbles. A fourth, siltstone, is made of silt. Silt is made of grains larger than mud but smaller than sand. A practical way of distinguishing these grain sizes is that sand is coarse enough to be seen with the naked eye, and most grains can be seen easily with a hand lens. Most grains in siltstone are too small to be seen with a hand lens, but the material still feels gritty. That's the standard that geologists use.

Sediment settles at different rates, depending on size. This lab allows you to experiment with a mixture of water and sediment and to actually record the deposition of particles by size. You should find that the largest, heaviest particles fall first, with the finer, lighter particles settling out last.

Materials

1   Pop bottle with cap, 2-liter
1   Pile of dirt, mud, sand, and pebbles
1   Metric ruler
1   Pencil
    Water

Procedure

1. Collect an assortment of sediment. Find some mud or fine, silty soil, some sand, a couple of pebbles, clay, spider lint, and other assorted sediments. Place them in the 2-liter pop bottle. You should have enough to fill up a third of the bottle.

2. With the collection of sediment now in the bottom of the bottle, fill the bottle with water and screw on the cap.

3. Shake vigorously. This will suspend the sediment in the water. Set the bottle on the table and allow it to stand undisturbed for 15 minutes. Observe the clarity of the water in the bottle at one-minute intervals.

4. After the sediment has settled, measure, in centimeters, the height of each visible layer. Record your measurements and draw your findings on the next page.

Conglomerate Stew

Data & Observations

Once the sediment has completely settled, draw a picture of your 2-liter bottle in the space below. Use the patterns identified below to separate the layers that you see, measure the height of each layer in centimeters, and record your measurements in the spaces in the key.

Silt / Clay_____ (cm)

Fine Sand_____ (cm)

Coarse Sand_____ (cm)

Gravel_____ (cm)

Rock Profile: Mudstone

How Was It Formed?

Mudstone is composed of the smallest sediment particles that are, by geological definition, 1/256 mm or smaller. These particles settle on top of one another for millions of years, layer after layer, and eventually the pressure caused by the weight of the sediment on the top of the pile drives the water out  near the bottom, causing some of the minerals to recrystallize. What was once squishy, gooey mud at the bottom of an ancient ocean or pond is now stone. Because these mud particles are so fine, they do not settle out of the water and onto the bottom of the seafloor or pond unless it is very still and there is little or no movement. This condition can exist in ponds, lagoons, and estuaries, but the most important environment for depositing large layers of mudstone is several miles offshore, where the wave action is diminished and the water is still. Mudstone is very similar in appearance to siltstone. The difference is that mudstone feels slippery when wet, and siltstone feels gritty. Also, geologists have an impromptu field test, not necessarily endorsed by the American Dental Association, where they bite off a small piece of the rock with their front teeth. If the sample feels slippery, it's mudstone. If it feels gritty, it's siltstone. If you have broken teeth, you've probably picked up a piece of metamorphic rock and you ought to think about another career.

What's It Used For?

Mudstone is used as a source of clay for ceramics, in construction as a component of cement, and as a filler in paint coatings. Some glossy papers are also produced using the fine sediments from mudstone.

Conglomerate Stew

Where Can I Find It?

Most of the interior of North America has been covered by inland seas at one time or another for the past millions of years, so mudstone is very abundant. It is commonly found sandwiched between limestone and dolomite formations anywhere from the Appalachians to the Rockies, throughout the Colorado Plateau, and in selected locations in the Great Basin.

Rock Profile: Siltstone

How Was It Formed?

Siltstone is composed of the next-smallest particles of sediment that are, by definition, smaller than 1/16 mm but larger than 1/256 mm. Like clay, which makes mudstone, these particles stay suspended in the water with the least amount of agitation or movement from waves or stream currents. Once the water bearing the silt reaches a relatively still portion  of a lake or ocean, the sediment will fall to the bottom and settle. Millions of years of this produces a finely layered rock.

While we are in the mudstone and siltstone section, we ought to properly define the term **shale**. This term is often used improperly to describe any rock that splits into flat layers. However, in the strictest sense of the word, shale is a mudstone or siltstone that splits into even, bedded layers.

What's It Used For?

Not much, except in rare places like Fossil Butte National Monument and the surrounding area where your specimen might have come from. About 50 million years ago, the area that is now Western Wyoming was a lush, humid, subtropical region with large lakes, lots of insects, plants, and fish.

Today, the land is dry and arid, and sits at a 7,000-foot-plus elevation. This is very different from the conditions during the Eocene Epoch, but it is known the world over for its abundant and beautiful fish fossils that are preserved in the fine silt layers. The sediment that is found in the area contributed to the preservation of animals and plants that fell into the lake and were buried. The sediment prevented much oxygen from reaching the dead fish or plants. As a result, the specimens were covered and preserved in excellent condition before they could decay. Because the sediment was deposited in layers and then hardened into rock, this is a true shale that does split evenly into very flat plates, very often exposing beautiful fossil specimens of not only fish but also insects, plants, snakes, crocodiles, turtles, monkeys, and water birds.

Where Can I Find It?

Siltstone is not quite as abundant as mudstone, but it is still common in areas where sedimentary rocks are found. Our favorite example is Fossil Butte, which produces thousands of the fish fossil, *Knightia sp.*, every year.

Rock Profile: Sandstone

How Was It Formed?

Sandstone is composed of sand particles that can be anywhere from 2 mm down to 1/16 mm in diameter. It can be found in any warm color, like yellow, tan, cream, red, orange, brown, or maroon, but it is not uncommon to find green samples of sandstone, as well. In this particular instance, your sandstone is red because it is full of rusty iron minerals.

Conglomerate Stew

The rock could have formed in a number of ways. It may have been piled up by the action of waves or wind along ancient shorelines, or deposited by streams and rivers. In either case, once the sand was deposited, it was pressed into a hard rock by sand or sediment that was later deposited on top of it.

What's It Used For?

Sandstone is used in walkways, gardens, and around fireplaces. If the banding patterns are particularly attractive, the rock can be cut and displayed as bookends, spheres, and as decorative freeform sculptures. Occasionally, rare forms of sandstone are quarried and used as a source of silica for the manufacture of glass, but it is more common to use loose sand for that purpose.

Sandstone is also very useful in helping geologists reconstruct the history of the Earth. If the sand grains are all the same size, then the sample probably had its origin in a wind-blown area full of sand dunes. If the grain size varies a little, it is an indication of an ancient shoreline deposit. Finally, if there is a huge range in the grain sizes, this would indicate that the layer of rock was probably deposited by a flood.

Where Can I Find It?

The area of the United States known as the Grand Staircase is composed of Bryce Canyon, Zion Canyon, and Grand Canyon National Parks. From top (Bryce) to bottom (Grand Canyon), it is the most complete geological record in one place on Earth.

Rock Profile: Conglomerate

How Was It Formed?

As you can tell from your specimen, this rock looks a lot like man-made
concrete. Conglomerate, by definition,
is composed of a random mixture of
pebbles, cemented together with clay,
mud, or sand and mineral matter. Another way to think of conglomerate is
like a great big, giant stew that was
cooked up by Ma Nature. She took
every kind of sediment and mixed it

together, didn't wait for everything to settle out the way it wanted to,
and then served up another layer of mud on top of it to seal it off.
Pieces of rock the size of pebbles or larger are transported from one
place to another by large, fast-moving rivers and streams, or by the
movement of ocean currents. Ancient shorelines of large lakes,
oceans, and some river channels collected sediment this size that was
later buried and solidified to form a conglomerate. Also, glaciers are
capable of not only moving large boulders but crushing and depositing them in piles called moraines that are later buried and compressed
into conglomerate. Because quite a bit of energy is required to move
pebbles and cobbles of any size, conglomerate is less common than
sandstone.

What's It Used For?

Occasionally, conglomerate is quarried and used as a source of
gravel or road base, but it is usually easier to use gravels in river
bottoms for this purpose. Because it is very porous, like sandstone,
conglomerate is an important source of oil, gas, and water.

Where Can I Find It?

It is most common near ancient mountain ranges, the Appalachians, on either side of the Rockies, and along the Pacific Coast.

Conglomerate Stew

How Come, Huh?

As wind and water erode existing mountains and volcanos, the sediment is washed or blown into low-lying areas where it accumulates. The first action is a destructive force, as the mountains are being dismantled, one piece of sediment at a time. The second is a constructive force. As the sediment piles up, it compacts into rock. As the Earth continues to move, plates shift and landforms change, and these rocks become exposed and form plateaus, canyons, escarpments, and hoo doos. Once they are exposed, the wind and water starts in on them again, and the whole process repeats.

Science Fair Extensions

61. Collect samples of sediment from several different sources: streambeds, river bottoms, lake bottoms, farm fields, construction sites, ocean shores, or flood plains of rivers and streams. Repeat the experiment and record the percentages of different kinds of sediment.

Dig It! • Lockwood DeWitt & B. K. Hixson

Sedimentary Rock Review

Geologically Speaking ...

This group of rocks is produced from pieces of other rocks. There are three classifications of sedimentary rocks:

A. Organic (oar • gan • ick) Sedimentary Rocks. **This group is produced when living matter dies, piles up, and then is compressed into rock.** When plants do this, we call the resulting material coal. When lots of sea animals with hard shells do this, we call the resulting material coquina.

B. Chemical (chem• uh • kull) Sedimentary Rocks. **These rocks are formed in several different ways. One way is when sea water, loaded with dissolved minerals, evaporates.** If you have ever swum in the ocean and then run around to dry off in the sun, you probably noticed you had salt crystals all over your skin. Imagine huge puddles of water, full of salt, drying up. The water would disappear into the air, but the salt would be left behind as a thick, white deposit.

C. Clastic (clahs • tick) Sedimentary Rocks. This is probably the group that most people think of when they talk about sedimentary rocks. **These are made up of pieces of other rocks that are deposited into layers by water or wind and then smooshed into rock.** All those mesas you see in the Wile E. Coyote cartoons are sedimentary rocks. This kind of rock is classified strictly by the size of the particles. The smallest particles are called clay, then silt, sand produces sandstone, and pebbles mixed with other sediments make up the last group, called conglomerates.

Sedimentary Rock Review

Materials

1   Piece of coal
1   Piece of halite
1   Piece of dolomite
1   Hand lens
1   Pencil

Procedure

1.   First, examine each of the sedimentary rocks in your collection with your hand lens. The coal is black, the halite is a reddish-white to cream color, and the dolomite is variable, from cream to dark-gray to black. It often has a very gritty texture, like sediment. On separate sheets of paper, draw pictures of each rock. Be sure to label your drawings.

2.   Examine all three rock samples and determine if a) the rock is made up mostly of fossils or b) the rock is brown to black and lighter in weight than you would expect for a rock. If your answer is "yes," this is most likely classified as an organic sedimentary rock. If you are still stumped at this point, grab the black rock. It is coal, which is made out of compressed leaves and other organic matter.

3.   Sort through the rocks again and find one that consists mostly of particles of sand or pebbles, or one that seems like it's made of mud or grit. It may help to use a hand lens. When you have found one, this is probably a clastic sedimentary rock. If the particles are large enough to be examined individually with the lens, see if they're little bits of fossil. This rock is called dolomite and is made up of mud-sized particles, which can be seen with the naked eye.

4. Sort through the rocks again and find one that consists mostly of obvious crystals or one that seems to consist of a single light-colored material. You have probably narrowed this down to your last sample, which is gypsum, a chemical sedimentary rock. This rock was formed when a large inland sea, full of salt, dried up. All of the water evaporated into the atmosphere, leaving behind the chemical salts, gypsum in this case, that hardened and formed a thick layer of rock.

Data & Observations

On a separate sheet of paper, draw a picture of each rock named in the boxes below. Be sure to label each of your drawings.

Sort your rocks into three groups. They will either be made of dead plant and animal matter (organic), from pieces of larger rocks that have been crushed and cemented together (clastic), or produced when large bodies of mineral-rich water dried up, leaving a thick deposit (evaporite). You have one of each, below:

Rock Name	Description	Type
Coal		
Halite		
Dolomite		

Sedimentary Rock Review

Sedimentary rocks are classified into three groups—clastic, evaporative, and organic—depending on how they were formed. In the table below, we provide a summary of the different specimens, along with their characteristics. When you are fairly certain that you have these ideas tucked firmly under your belt, move on to the metamorphics.

Rock Type	Characteristics	Samples
Clastic	Formed by sediment being deposited Rock fragments or grains visible Grain size determines the name Grains are angular or round	Conglomerate Mudstone Siltstone Sandstone

Chemical	Formed when mineral-rich
	    waters precipitate
	Crystals interlocking, usually
	    one mineral
	Rock appears to have layers or bands
		Geyserite
		
		Halite
		
		Gypsum
		Dolomite

Organic	Formed from fossil plants Formed from fossil shells	Coal Coquina

Big Idea 10

Metamorphic rocks started out as one kind of rock—igneous, sedimentary, or metamorphic—but got squished, heated, and changed into new rocks.

Dissolving Statues

Geologically Speaking ...

One of the big environmental problems facing the Eastern United States and much of Europe is acid rain. The big factories and automobiles belch out gases that go into the air, and when mixed with rain, produce acidic solutions. One consequence of this is that marble, which is made out of calcite (calcium carbonate), reacts with dilute acid. In other words, it dissolves. If the problem goes unchecked, we will have statues that look like they are slowly melting as the years pass. This lab will demonstrate the effect of dilute acid on marble.

Materials

1   Drinking glass, 8 oz.
1   Bottle of distilled, white vinegar
1   Sample of marble
1   Hand lens or magnifier

Procedure

1. Place the piece of marble in the glass. Fill the glass with vinegar to a level that is one inch above the top of the marble.

2. After a minute or two, examine the marble with the hand lens. You should see small bubbles. This is carbon dioxide gas, being produced on the surface of the rock. Vinegar is a very weak acid. When it comes in contact with the calcium carbonate in the marble, it reacts to produce the gas. A very fine sediment is also produced as a by-product of the reaction. If you let the reaction continue, the marble will dissolve completely.

3. To save your marble from eventual disintegration, remove it from the glass and rinse it with water. The alternative, of course, is to let the reaction run its course, in which case, you can say "adios" to your marble.

4. Compare your results to those obtained earlier with coquina and dolomite. It would be interesting to see what would happen if artists started carving statues out of dolomite and then they were exposed to acid rain.

How Come, Huh?

Marble is formed when limestone or dolomite is heated and squished in the traditional, metamorphic rock manner. Just as quartzite forms when "clean" sandstone is metamorphosed, marble forms from pure limestone or dolomite. Limestone is basically a rock made of calcite (calcium carbonate), and the rock dolomite is made out of the mineral dolomite (magnesium carbonate). With only one mineral present in either of these rocks, new minerals are not formed when metamorphosis starts. However, as is the case with quartzite, the calcite and dolomite recrystallize, grow larger, and fill in any holes in the original rock. The difference is that both calcite and dolomite recrystallize quickly and easily, which gives marble very large crystal grains. Also, the chemical bonds in marble are quite weak when compared to those of most other minerals. As a result, marble breaks, bends, and folds very easily compared to other rocks during the process of metamorphosis. You could say that marble is the Silly Putty of the rock world.

Dissolving Statues

Rock Profile: Quartzite

How Was It Formed?

Quartzite is formed when a "clean" quartz sandstone is metamorphosed. **Clean** is a term used by geologists to describe rocks made of sand, with very little clay, mud, or other goobers.

When quartz is metamorphosed, the quartz grains grow together, spaces between the sand grains collapse under the pressure, and small grains are absorbed by larger grains. Even though the characteristics of the rock are largely unchanged, there are still enough differences that make quartzite readily distinguishable from a clean, quartz-rich sandstone.

Grab the red sandstone specimen from the sedimentary section. We are going to use it for comparison. When you handle a piece of sandstone, grains will normally crumble off if you rub the side of the rock. Quartzite, on the other hand, has been exposed to incredible temperature and pressure and, as a result, is cemented together well with interlocking grains. This means that the grains cannot be rubbed or knocked off easily. Sandstone appears somewhat porous, with many small holes between the grains. In quartzite, these holes are almost completely filled with recrystallized quartz. As a result, the rock is not porous at all and feels somewhat heavier than a similar-sized piece of sandstone. Finally, quartzite is very hard and durable, so it weathers and erodes very slowly.

What's It Used For?

Quartzite is useful as a source of pure quartz, and is used for making glass. Because of its durability and purity, it is useful as road base gravel for road building, and you may even find crushed pieces in the bottom of your aquarium.

Where Can I Find It?

Quartzite is fairly common in areas of mountain-building, such as the Appalachian, Wasatch, and Rocky Mountains.

Rock Profile: Marble

How Was It Formed?

An important point is that dolomite and calcite tend to form large, 3-dimensional crystals during metamorphosis, rather than flat or needle-shaped crystals. Because of this, marble (and quartzite too, for that matter) do not show the tendency to develop strong rock cleavage the way that rocks with platy minerals do. So even though limestone, dolomite, and clean sandstone may be subjected to the same conditions as mudstones and siltstones, they do not turn into foliated metamorphic rocks.

What's It Used For?

Marble is cut and polished very easily and comes in several attractive colors and patterns. Given these characteristics, marble is used extensively as a building stone. It is also widely used for tabletops and countertops, sculptures, floor tiles, and lavatories.

Where Can I Find It?

New Hampshire and Vermont are famous for their marble quarries. Marble is also common throughout the Appalachian Mountains, the Rocky Mountain states, in metamorphic rocks of the Basin and Range of Nevada, and in Eastern California.

Science Fair Extensions

62. Report on acid rain, how it occurs, where it is most common, what is being done to combat it, and if there are any effects in your community.

63. Repeat the experiment with a piece of calcite and compare the results. Be prepared to explain why the calcite reacts the way it does. Do a little research to see if there are other rocks and/or minerals that react with dilute acid.

Sediment to Schist

Geologically Speaking ...

As a sedimentary rock undergoes increasing degrees of metamorphosis, its shape, texture, and color change. This lab will demonstrate how sedimentary rock changes from mudstone to slate with a little bit of pressure, then to phyllite with more pressure, and finally to schist under conditions of extreme pressure, not to mention heat that would annoy even the Volcano Gods.

Materials

1   Piece of aluminum foil, approx. 12 inches by 12 inches
1   Hammer
1   Hard, flat surface that you can pound on
1   Hand lens
1   Pair of goggles
1   Sample of slate
1   Sample of phyllite
1   Sample of schist

Procedure

1. Take the foil and gently wad it up into a ball. Examine the foil. You should be able to see that it has been folded into thousands of nearly-flat surfaces. Some of these surfaces are curved, but most are flat surfaces that point in every direction. If you were to look at the flakes of clay in a freshly deposited glob of sediment, they would look something like the surfaces in your aluminum ball.

2. Now, take the ball and press it against the table. Flip it over and press on it as hard as you can. Examine the foil. You should still see many flat surfaces, pointing in many different directions, but now one direction is more common than others. As your glob of sediment changes from loose particles to a rock, the flat mineral grains tend to line up with one another.

3. Take the hammer and gently pound the foil until it is about half as thick as the original. Take another peek. You'll see that most surfaces are lined up parallel to one another. As a sedimentary rock is metamorphosed into slate and then into phyllite, two important things happen. First, flat minerals line up parallel to one another and, second, the flat particles of clay start to recrystallize into flat particles of mica.

4. Now, take the hammer and mash the foil as hard as you can. Pick up the remains and look at the result. Notice that it is almost impossible to find a surface anywhere that is not parallel to the others. The original shape of your "sediment" has all but disappeared. In fact, the foil may be coming apart in pieces now because the blows of the hammer force the foil to squish out sideways, which is a process called "shearing." You have now created a "rock" similar to schist. All the mineral grains are parallel, and very little of the original form remains.

Sediment to Schist

Data & Observations

In the spaces that are provided below, draw pictures of the foil after it has been mashed with your hands, whapped with the hammer, and completely smashed with the hammer. Label each section.

Rock Profile: Slate

How Was It Formed?

Slate is the rock first formed as a result of increasing temperature and pressure. In rocks with a fair amount of clay (siltstone and mudstone), the minerals in the clay will start to slowly transform into mica. The mica grows perpendicular to the direction of greatest compressive force. Imagine you have a pile of paper between your hands. If you start pushing your  hands together with greater force, the paper will conform to the force between your hands and flatten out parallel to your palms, or perpendicular to the force. The same process happens during metamorphosis. The clay minerals, which are flat to begin with, will turn so that the flat sides are perpendicular to the compression. The new minerals that grow, like mica, grow with their flat sides perpendicular to the compression. This feature—the flat sides of minerals perpendicular to the greatest compression—is characteristic of all the foliated metamorphic rocks. To take it one step further, minerals that are needle-like in form, like hornblende, will grow so that the needles are also perpendicular to compression. Another way of thinking about this process is that the minerals grow in the direction of least compression.

The distinguishing characteristic of slate is that most of the mineral grains are too small to see with the naked eye or even with a hand lens. Slate is generally a monotone-gray to earthy-green, and is typically dark in tone. So how can you tell that the mineral grains are lined up? Another distinguishing feature of slate is its tendancy to break into flat sheets. This is similar to mineral cleavage, so it's frequently referred to as rock cleavage. All those tiny mica grains are lined up, and all of them tend to split parallel to their flat sides. So when the rock splits, the fracture takes advantage of the weakness in all the parallel mica grains and follows those planes. That means that the rock splits along nice, flat surfaces.

Sediment to Schist

What's It Used For?

Slate's dark color and ease of splitting lead to most of its uses: It is used for roofing, blackboards, paving flagstones, as a decorative facing stone, and for kitchen and bathroom counter surfaces.

Many of these uses are becoming less common as synthetic substitutes take over. Blackboards, for example, are almost entirely made of fiberboard cemented by a petroleum-based binder; these are lighter in weight, and have a smoother, more even surface. Roofing tiles are made of a similar material. Nevertheless, slate will always have the appeal of its natural texture, and although it is relatively heavy, it's a fairly inexpensive material to work with.

Where Can I Find It?

Slate is found in areas of moderate to low metamorphosis, for example, surrounding the cores of intense mountain-building activity. It is abundant in the Appalachian Mountains, in the Rockies, and in mountainous areas of the west.

Rock Profile: Phyllite

How Was It Formed?

Phyllite is produced when sedimentary rock is heated and squished to form a harder, more durable rock. The minerals making up the original rock melt and recrystallize to form new minerals. Some of the first minerals to appear are members of the mica group, which are shiny, flat, flaky minerals. This gives the rock a texture, or fabric, that is dominated by the millions of parallel mica flakes. Mica splits easily along its flat surfaces. As a consequence, the whole rock splits parallel to the mica grains, producing a flat rock with a glossy surface.

Slate forms under mild metamorphic conditions. Schist forms under moderate metamorphic conditions. In between, we have phyllite, so it can be difficult to distinguish phyllite from slate and schist. Slate tends to be darker and does not have the silvery sheen of phyllite. However, it may have a bit of a glossy appearance. Most of the mineral grains in schist are large enough to see.

What's It Used For?

Phyllite is often recruited to become flagstones for walkways, especially when a fair amount of quartz is present to give the rock hardness and durability. It is also used as an architectural stone, especially for interior stonework, like in fireplaces, and for garden stonework, including walkways, walls, and raised flower beds.

Where Can I Find It?

Phyllite is common in areas of moderate metamorphosis, but is replaced by schist or gneiss in mountain core areas.

Rock Profile: Schist

How Was It Formed?

The inside of the Earth is very hot and under a lot of pressure. When rock that is rich in sediment (sand, clay, or mud) gets buried deep inside this kind of environment, the minerals start to recrystallize. Sand grains, composed of quartz and feldspar, recrystallize to form larger grains of quartz and feldspar.

Sediment to Schist

Clay and mud, when heated under great pressure, create mica, a type of mineral that forms flat, shiny sheets. These sheets will grow perpendicular to the direction of the greatest force pushing down on them. Imagine squishing a lump of clay with a flat hand. The hand pushed down but the clay squished out perpendicular to the pressure that you put on it with your hand. Mica forms in the same way.

At the same time that these minerals are recrystallizing, compression and shearing gently kneads the rock like bread dough. The mica tends to cluster together in one set of layers, and the quartz and feldspar settle in another. This kneading creates a layered appearance of dark and light bands of crystals called **foliation**. Because mica grains tend to split easily along their flat surfaces, the abundance of the mineral mica in a schist sample means that the rock will split easily.

Schist and phyllite are similar looking, but most of the mineral grains in phyllite, with the exception of mica, are too small to be seen. Schist, on the other hand, has other minerals that have formed at higher pressure, such as ruby-red garnet and light-blue kyanite. If not visible to the naked eye, a hand lens should reveal these additional minerals. Also, because of the additional stress it was under, schist does not split as easily into flat, layered pieces.

What's It Used For?

Schist is fairly common and easy to find, but it has very few properties that make it useful commercially. Occasionally, certain minerals, such as garnet or graphite, are present in large enough quantities that schist is mined for them, but, overall, the rock is too fragile for construction or building purposes.

Where Can I Find It?

Schist is very common in mountainous areas like the Appalachians in the east and the Sierra Nevadas in the west. It is also found in several western mountain chains and is present in areas where erosion has cut down into older rocks. The Grand Canyon is our favorite example of erosion gone wild.

Science Fair Extensions

64. Take four pieces of foil and prepare models of sediment, mudstone, phyllite, and schist. Place the models next to actual samples with descriptions of how the metamorphic process affects each one.

Foliated Clay Cakes

Geologically Speaking ...

This lab gives you the opportunity to see how pressure can produce mineral foliation in metamorphic rocks. You will compare a sample of quartz monzonite and your beginning lump of clay to a sample of gneiss and your ending lump of clay.

Materials

1   Rolling pin
1   Lump of clay
     Rice, 1/2 c.
1   Sample of quartz monzonite
1   Sample of gneiss

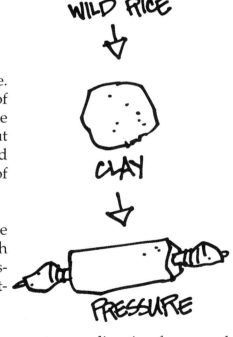

WILD RICE

CLAY

PRESSURE

Procedure

1.   Pour the rice onto the table. Roll the ball of clay in the rice. Some of the rice will stick to the outside of the clay. Knead it until the rice is spread out fairly evenly. Roll the ball again and repeat until the clay sample has lots of "minerals" distributed throughout.

2.   Using the rolling pin, roll the clay out so that it is about 1/4-inch thick. Don't roll it with too much pressure. The grains of rice should be pointing in lots of different directions.

3.   Roll and fold the clay in the exact same direction for several minutes. Flatten the lump to a 1/4-inch thickness. You should notice that the rice grains are, for the most part, lined up in parallel lines.

4.   Think of the kneaded clay as quartz monzonite and the rolled clay as gneiss. Compare the two.

Data & Observations

In the spaces that are provided below, draw pictures of quartz monzonite and gneiss.

How Come, Huh?

As a result of doing this activitiy, you should see that when pressure is applied to the clay, the rice grains, which represent minerals in the rock, start to line up or form foliations and bands. This is what happens under conditions of metamorphosis. As the quartz monzonite is heated and exposed to pressure, the minerals begin to grow, recrystallize, and realign themselves in bands or foliations. The end-product is gneiss.

Foliated Clay Cakes

Rock Profile: Gneiss

How Was It Formed?

Gneiss (nice) is the very end-product for rocks that have been heated to very high temperatures and smashed under tons and tons of pressure. It has two possible origins. First, it may have started out as sedimentary rock and changed as it went through the metamorphic stages: slate to phyllite, phyllite to schist, and schist to gneiss. We covered this in the last lab. Second, granites or other igneous rocks could have changed to gneiss when they were exposed to high temperatures and pressures.

In some samples, it is very difficult to tell which origin is correct. If the metamorphic conditions had been much more extreme, meaning higher temperatures and pressures, the rock would have melted, turning into magma, and then cooled to form an igneous rock. Because of this, gneiss can look quite similar to granite. Generally, the banding of light and dark minerals, called the rock's fabric, is easy to spot and gives geologists a method to separate the two. Gneiss can also look a lot like schist. However, it doesn't split into nice, flat layers but, rather, produces a blocky, irregular fracture. This difference is due to the fact that gneiss has less mica. Because very high temperatures and pressures are necessary to create gneiss, the rock becomes very soft and mooshy. When it finally hardens, the even, flat, mineral beds have been squished and twisted into wavy, swirled bands. Take a gander at the photo for a good example.

What's It Used For?

Gneiss comes in a wide variety of attractive colors and patterns and is used extensively as an architectural stone, providing beautiful patterns to the outsides of buildings. Also, gneiss is quarried and used for road base and fill for railroad tracks.

Where Can I Find It?

Gneiss is common in the Appalachians, throughout the Rocky Mountains, and in deeply-eroded, ancient mountain areas, such as the bottom of the Grand Canyon. The most extensive areas of gneiss are found in the Canadian Shield.

Science Fair Extensions

65. Collect a whole series of foliated metamorphic rocks and show the gradual increase in deformation that leads to the production of these kinds of rocks.

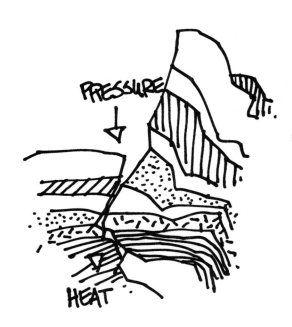

Metamorphic Rock Review

Geologically Speaking ...

Metamorphic rocks start out as one kind of rock—igneous, sedimentary, or metamorphic—but get squished, heated, and changed into a new rocks. This happens because, under tremendous heat and pressure found inside the Earth, atoms and molecules that make up the original minerals in the original rocks start to move around and recombine to form new minerals and crystals. However, unlike igneous rocks, the conditions are not hot enough to make the rocks melt. The conditions that allow this to happen are as follows:

1. The Earth's tectonic plates run into one another and build mountain ranges.
2. The Earth's tectonic plates slide past one another.
3. Molten rock heats nearby solid rocks.
4. Sediments get buried very deep.

This lab introduces you to the two groups of metamorphic rocks, **foliated**, or layered, and **non-foliated**, or uniform in texture and color.

Materials

1   Piece of marble
1   Hand lens
1   Piece of phyllite
1   Pencil (student)
1   Piece of quartzite
1   Bottle of vinegar, 2 oz.
1   Pipette

Procedure

1. Separating Foliated from Non-Foliated Rocks.

The word "foliation" comes from the root word meaning "leaf," the same root as "foliage," and refers to the arrangement of minerals into thin layers.

Examine each sample for layered patterns. This layering may show up as a fracture pattern that breaks into thin sheets, bands of different-colored minerals, bands running through the sample, or as a mineral grain alignment with all the mica flakes running parallel to one another. If you observe any of the properties listed, you probably have a foliated, metamorphic sample.

2. Identifying the Different Kinds of Foliated Rocks.

You can now identify foliated samples by comparing them to the descriptions below:

a. If the sample is dark-gray to black and has no or very few visible crystals, it is <u>slate</u>.

b. If the sample is silvery- or glossy-gray to green, with few crystals visible to the naked eye but with many individual grains (or little sparkles) visible with magnification, it is <u>phyllite</u>.

c. If the sample has most grains visible to the naked eye, many flat minerals (mica), and/or long, thin, needlelike crystals, and if little, sparkly bits often come off onto your hands, it is <u>schist</u>.

d. If the sample has all crystals easily visible with the naked eye, some flat and needlelike crystals but not a lot, and if it looks like granite with colored bands and does not pick apart easily, it is <u>gneiss</u>.

This sequence (slate➞phyllite➞schist➞gneiss) represents progressively higher temperatures and pressures. As the temperature and pressure increase, mineral grains grow larger, line up better, and eventually start changing from flat or needle-shaped to increasingly 3–dimensional.

Metamorphic Rock Review

3. **Examining Your Non-Foliated Rocks.**

It's time to evaluate samples that you think are non-foliated. Ask the following questions of your rocks, and don't get too whacked if they don't answer back right away:

    a. Is the sample pretty much the same all over?

    b. Does it seem to be composed of just one substance?

    c. Does it lack a layered texture <u>or</u> does it have color bands that appear to be the same material as elsewhere, but are a slightly different color?

If you answered "yes" to these questions, you probably have a non-foliated metamorphic rock. Please note that both foliated and non-foliated metamorphic rocks may have distinct color bands. In non-foliated rocks, these bands come from slightly different compositions in the original bedding. In foliated rocks, these bands come from recrystallization and mineral separation. So, if you're still not certain, compare the colored bands to the rest of the rock. Are they the same <u>except</u> for color? If the different colored bands seem to be pretty much the same except for color, call the sample "non-foliated."

4. Identifying the Different Kinds of Non-Foliated Rocks.

You can now identify non-foliated samples by comparing them to the descriptions below:

a. If the sample is easily scratched with a penny and the sample bubbles slowly when you drop vinegar on it: <u>marble</u> (metamorphosed limestone).

b. If the sample can scratch a penny and a glass plate, is light in color (normally), and is made of sand-sized or larger grains: <u>quartzite</u> (metamorphosed sandstone).

c. If the sample is very fine-grained, scratches a penny and may or may not scratch glass very well: <u>argillite</u> or <u>hornfels</u> (metamorphosed mudstone). These two rocks are very similar in appearance and are difficult to distinguish from each other without knowing where they came from.

Data & Observations

Sort your rocks into groups by whether they are foliated or non-foliated rocks. Fill in the data table below with the appropriate information.

Rock Name	Description	Type
Marble		
Phyllite		
Quartzite		

Metamorphic Rock Review

Metamorphic rocks are classified into two groups, **foliated** and **non-foliated**. In the event that you have been sleeping through the last ten pages or so, a foliation is a band, or streak, of mineral that is created when the original rock is heated and squished. As this happens, the minerals in the rock recrystallize perpendicular to the force that is being placed on them.

After you have separated the rocks into foliated and non-foliated groups, the foliated rocks can be arranged in order of increasing metamorphism. The tables below should help to clarify the information.

Foliated & Non-Foliated Metamorphics

Rock Type	Characteristics	Samples
Foliated	Crystals present in bands or layers Micas appear to be ordered	Phyllite Schist Gneiss
Non-Foliated	Crystals interlocking, usually one mineral No layers or bands Rocks appear to have been melted or transformed	Soapstone Quartzite Marble

Dig It! • *Lockwood DeWitt & B. K. Hixson*

& Mashed Sediment Menu

Pre and Post Metamorphic Rocks

Rock Type	Samples	Metamorphosed to
Sedimentary	Mudstone	Phyllite
Sedimentary	Limestone/Coquina	Marble
Sedimentary	Sandstone	Quartzite
Igneous	Granite	Gneiss

Increasingly Metamorphosed Mudstone

Conditions	Rock Formed
No Heat or Pressure	Mudstone
Initial Heat & Pressure	Slate
Moderate Heat & Pressure	Phyllite
Extreme Heat & Pressure	Schist
Radical Heat & Mondo Pressure	Gneiss

The Rock Cycle

Congratulations! You've made it to the end of the book. Forty-two lab activities later, we would like to present one final challenge to you that connects all of the rocks to one another. This idea is called a **rock cycle** and is pictured below. We have added all of the major events. Your task is to draw arrows showing how each rock group is related to every other rock group. We have inserted one arrow, and now your job is to figure out all of the other possible relationships.

Igneous

Weathering &
Erosion

Weathering &
Erosion

Weathering &
Erosion

Sedimentary

Compaction &
Cementation

You can start at any point and wind up back where you started. For example, mud may settle into the bottom of a lake and get smooshed into mudstone. The mudstone gets buried even further and, under the pressure and heat of the Earth, forms slate. Mountain-building in the general area shoves the slate to the core of the Earth, where it is melted, forming magma that erupts onto the surface of the Earth as pumice. The pumice erodes over time and forms fine particles resembling mud as they are washed downstream into a lake bottom … and so it goes.

Cooling

Melting

Melting

Heat &
Pressure

Metamorphic

Heat &
Pressure

Science Fair Projects
•
A Step-by-Step Guide: From Idea to Presentation

Dig It! • Lockwood DeWitt & B. K. Hixson

Science Fair Projects

Ah, the impending science fair project—a good science fair project has the following five characteristics:

1. The student must come up with an *original* question.
2. That *original* question must be suited to an experiment in order to provide an answer.
3. The *original* idea is outlined with just one variable isolated.
4. The *original* experiment is performed and documented using the scientific method.
5. A presentation of the *original* idea in the form of a lab write-up and display board is completed.

Science Fair Projects

As simple as science fair versus science project sounds, it gets screwed up millions of times a year by sweet, unsuspecting students who are counseled by sweet, unknowing, and probably just as confused parents.

To give you a sense of contrast we have provided a list of legitimate science fair projects and then reports that do not qualify. We will also add some comments in italics that should help clarify why they do or do not qualify in the science fair project department.

Science Fair Projects

1. Temperature and the amount of time it takes mealworms to change to beetles.

Great start. We have chosen a single variable that is easy to measure: temperature. From this point forward the student can read, explore, and formulate an original question that is the foundation for the project.

A colleague of mine actually did a similar type of experiment for his master's degree. His topic: The rate of development of fly larva in cow poop as a function of temperature. No kidding. He found out that the warmer the temperature of the poop the faster the larva developed into flies.

2. The effect of different concentrations of soapy water on seed germination.

Again, wonderful. Measuring the concentration of soapy water. This leads naturally into original questions and a good project.

3. Crystal size and the amount of sugar in the solution.

This could lead into other factors such as exploring the temperature of the solution, the size of the solution container, and other variables that may affect crystal growth. Opens a lot of doors.

vs. Science Reports

4. Helicopter rotor size and the speed at which it falls.

Size also means surface area, which is very easy to measure. The student who did this not only found the mathematical threshold with relationship to air friction, but she had a ton of fun.

5. The ideal ratio of baking soda to vinegar to make a fire extinguisher.

Another great start. Easy to measure and track, leads to a logical question that can either be supported or refuted with the data.

Each of those topics *measures* one thing such as the amount of sugar, the concentration of soapy water, or the ideal size. If you start with an idea that allows you to measure something, then you can change it, ask questions, explore, and ultimately make a *prediction*, also called a *hypothesis*, and experiment to find out if you are correct. Here are some well-meaning but misguided entries:

Science Reports, <u>not Projects</u>
1. Dinosaurs!
OK, great. Everyone loves dinosaurs but where is the experiment? Did you find a new dinosaur? Is Jurassic Park alive and well, and we are headed there to breed, drug, or in some way test them? Probably not. This was a report on T. rex. Cool, but not a science fair project. And judging by the protest that this kid's mom put up when the kid didn't get his usual "A", it is a safe bet that she put a lot of time in and shared in the disappointment.

More Reports &

2. Our Friend the Sun

Another very large topic, no pun intended. This could be a great topic. Sunlight is fascinating. It can be split, polarized, reflected, refracted, measured, collected, converted. However, this poor kid simply chose to write about the size of the sun, regurgitating facts about its features, cycles, and other astrofacts while simultaneously offending the American Melanoma Survivors Society. Just kidding about that last part.

3. Smokers' Poll

A lot of folks think that they are headed in the right direction here. Again, it depends on how the kid attacks the idea. Are they going to single out race? Heredity? Shoe size? What exactly are they after here? The young lady who did this report chose to make it more of a psychology-studies effort than a scientific report. She wanted to know family income, if they fought with their parents, how much stress was on the job, and so on. All legitimate concerns but not placed in the right slot.

4. The Majestic Moose

If you went out and caught the moose, drugged it to see the side effects for disease control, or even mated it with an elk to determine if you could create an animal that would become the spokesanimal for the Alabama Dairy Farmers' Got Melk? promotion, that would be fine. But, another fact-filled report should be filed with the English teacher.

5. How Tadpoles Change into Frogs

Great start, but they forgot to finish the statement. We know how tadpoles change into frogs. What we don't know is how tadpoles change into frogs if they are in an altered environment, if they are hatched out of cycle, if they are stuck under the tire of an off-road vehicle blatantly driving through a protected wetland area. That's what we want to know. How tadpoles change into frogs, if, when, or under what measurable circumstances.

Now that we have beat the chicken squat out of this introduction, we are going to show you how to pick a topic that can be adapted to become a successful science fair project after one more thought.

One Final Comment

A Gentle Reminder

Quite often I discuss the scientific method with moms and dads, teachers and kids, and get the impression that, according to their understanding, there is one, and only one, scientific method. This is not necessarily true. There are lots of ways to investigate the world we live in and on.

Paleontologists dig up dead animals and plants but have no way to conduct experiments on them. They're dead. Albert Einstein, the most famous scientist of the last century and probably on everybody's starting five of all time, never did experiments. He was a theoretical physicist, which means that he came up with a hypothesis, skipped over collecting materials for things like black holes and space-time continuums, didn't experiment on anything or even collect data. He just went straight from hypothesis to conclusion, and he's still considered part of the scientific community. You'll probably follow the six steps we outline but keep an open mind.

Project Planner

This outline is designed to give you a specific set of timelines to follow as you develop your science fair project. Most teachers will give you 8 to 11 weeks notice for this kind of assignment. We are going to operate from the shorter timeline with our suggested schedule, which means that the first thing you need to do is get a calendar.

A. The suggested time to be devoted to each item is listed in parentheses next to that item. Enter the date of the Science Fair and then, using the calendar, work backward entering dates.

B. As you complete each item, enter the date that you completed it in the column between the goal (due date) and project item.

Goal   Completed   Project Item

1. Generate a Hypothesis (2 weeks)

_____ _____   Review Idea Section, pp. 191–198
_____ _____   Try Several Experiments
_____ _____   Hypothesis Generated
_____ _____   Finished Hypothesis Submitted
_____ _____   Hypothesis Approved

2. Gather Background Information (1 week)

_____ _____   Concepts/Discoveries Written Up
_____ _____   Vocabulary/Glossary Completed
_____ _____   Famous Scientists in Field

& Timeline

Goal   Completed   Project Item

3. Design an Experiment (1 week)

_____	_____	Procedure Written
_____	_____	Lab Safety Review Completed
_____	_____	Procedure Approved
_____	_____	Data Tables Prepared
_____	_____	Materials List Completed
_____	_____	Materials Acquired

4. Perform the Experiment (2 weeks)

_____	_____	Scheduled Lab Time

5. Collect and Record Experimental Data (part of 4)

_____	_____	Data Tables Completed
_____	_____	Graphs Completed
_____	_____	Other Data Collected and Prepared

6. Present Your Findings (2 weeks)

_____	_____	Rough Draft of Paper Completed
_____	_____	Proofreading Completed
_____	_____	Final Report Completed
_____	_____	Display Completed
_____	_____	Oral Report Outlined on Index Cards
_____	_____	Practice Presentation of Oral Report
_____	_____	Oral Report Presentation
_____	_____	Science Fair Setup
_____	_____	Show Time!

Scientific Method
• Step 1 •
The Hypothesis

The Hypothesis

A hypothesis is an educated guess. It is a statement of what you think will probably happen. It is also the most important part of your science fair project because it directs the entire process. It determines what you study, the materials you will need, and how the experiment will be designed, carried out, and evaluated. Needless to say, you need to put some thought into this part.

There are four steps to generating a hypothesis:

Step One • Pick a Topic
Preferably something that you are interested in studying. We would like to politely recommend that you take a peek at physical science ideas (physics and chemistry) if you are a rookie and this is one of your first shots at a science fair project. These kinds of lab ideas allow you to repeat experiments quickly. There is a lot of data that can be collected, and there is a huge variety to choose from.

If you are having trouble finding an idea, all you have to do is pick up a compilation of science activities (like this one) and start thumbing through it. Go to the local library or head to a bookstore and you will find a wide and ever-changing selection to choose from. Find a topic that interests you and start reading. At some point an idea will catch your eye, and you will be off to the races.

Pick a Topic . . .

We hope you find an idea you like between the covers of this book. But we also realize that 1) there are more ideas about geology than we have included in this book and 2) other kinds of presentations, or methods of writing labs, may be just what you need to trigger a new idea or put a different spin on things. So, without further ado, we introduce you to several additional titles that may be of help to you in developing a science fair project.

1. Simple Earth Science Experiments with Everyday Materials. Written by Louis V. Loeschnig. ISBN 0-8069-0898-X. Published by Sterling. 128 pages.

Nearly one hundred experiments using common household materials. This book covers earthquakes, phototropism, fossils, and heaps of other topics. A good all around book for covering the basics about the Earth and the world we live in. These experiments even come with entertaining illustrations.

2. Adventures with Rocks and Minerals, Book II. Written by Lloyd H. Barrow. ISBN 0-89490-164-8. Published by Enslow. 96 pages.

Thirty easy labs! This book even has edible experiments. These simple experiments illuminate the effects of erosion in several interesting ways. The experiments show the different reactions that furrows, plants, hard-packed soil, and even concrete have with water. If you enjoyed *Dig It!*, this book may be of interest to you.

3. Geology Rocks! Written by Cindy Blobaum. ISBN 1-885593-29-5. Published by Williamson. 96 pages.

Cindy gives us 50 hands-on science experiments geared for 7-14 year old students. This book is part of the Kaleidoscope Kids™ book series. This is a high energy book that has lots of pictures and is set up in a creative manner. This book covers a gamut of geological topics such as wells, acid rain, fossils, and volcanos.

Find an Idea You Like

4. The Earth Science Book. Written by Dinah Zike.
ISBN 0-471-57166-0. Published by John Wiley and Sons, Inc. 120 pages.

This starts with the earth's place in the universe, and then discusses the moon, with hands on experiments. Then the parts of the earth are demonstrated with more experiments. If you want a good, comprehensive book about the Earth with lots of experiments, this book might be for you.

5. Geology. Written by Grahm Peacock & Jill Jesson.
ISBN 1-56847-193-9. Published by Thomson Learning. 32 pages.

Geared for anklebiters, filled with color pictures and photographs. Thirteen simple experiments and equiped with a glossary. This will help them understand the geology basics. Your younger students should really enjoy this books.

6. Rocks and Minerals. Written by Janice VanCleave.
ISBN 0-471-10269-5. Published by John Wiley and Sons, Inc. 89 pages.

Over one million of Janice's books have been sold. This book has twenty hands-on science activities that cover homemade fossils, handmade crystals, and much more. Most of the experiments are geared to all ages of students.

Develop an Original Idea

Step Two • Do the Lab

Choose a lab activity that looks interesting and try the experiment. Some kids make the mistake of thinking that all you have to do is find a lab in a book, repeat the lab, and you are on the gravy train with biscuit wheels. Your goal is to ask an ORIGINAL question, not repeat an experiment that has been done a bazillion times before.

As you do the lab, be thinking not only about the data you are collecting, but of ways you could adapt or change the experiment to find out new information. The point of the science fair project is to have you become an actual scientist and contribute a little bit of new knowledge to the world.

You know that they don't pay all of those engineers good money to sit around and repeat other people's lab work. The company wants new ideas so if you are able to generate and explore new ideas you become very valuable, not only to that company but to society. It is the question-askers that find cures for diseases, create new materials, figure out ways to make existing machines energy efficient, and change the way that we live. For the purpose of illustration, we are going to take a lab titled, "Prisms, Water Prisms." from another book, *Photon U*, and run it through the rest of the process. The lab uses a tub of water, an ordinary mirror, and light to create a prism that splits the light into the spectrum of a rainbow. Cool. Easy to do. Not expensive and open to all kinds of adaptations, including the four that we discuss on the next page.

Step Three • Bend, Fold, Spindle, & Mutilate Your Lab

Once you have picked out an experiment, ask if it is possible to do any of the following things to modify it into an original experiment. You want to try and change the experiment to make it more interesting and find out one new, small piece of information.

Heat it	Freeze it	Reverse it	Double it
Bend it	Invert it	Poison it	Dehydrate it
Drown it	Stretch it	Fold it	Ignite it
Split it	Irradiate it	Oxidize it	Reduce it
Chill it	Speed it up	Color it	Grease it
Expand it	Substitute it	Remove it	Slow it down

If you take a look at our examples, that's exactly what we did to the main idea. We took the list of 24 different things that you could do to an experiment—not nearly all of them by the way—and tried a couple of them out on the prism setup.

Double it: Get a second prism and see if you can continue to separate the colors further by lining up a second prism in the rainbow of the first.

Reduce it: Figure out a way to gather up the colors that have been produced and mix them back together to produce white light again.

Reverse it: Experiment with moving the flashlight and paper closer to the mirror and farther away. Draw a picture and be able to predict what happens to the size and clarity of the rainbow image.

Substitute it: You can also create a rainbow on a sunny day using a garden hose with a fine-spray nozzle attached. Set the nozzle adjustment so that a fine mist is produced and move the mist around in the sunshine until you see the rainbow. This works better if the sun is lower in the sky; late afternoon is best.

Hypothesis Worksheet

Step Three (Expanded) • Bend, Fold, Spindle Worksheet

This worksheet will give you an opportunity to work through the process of creating an original idea.

A. Write down the lab idea that you want to mangle.

_____

_____

_____

_____

B. List the possible variables you could change in the lab.

    i. _____

    ii. _____

    iii. _____

    iv. _____

    v. _____

C. Take one variable listed in section B and apply one of the 24 changes listed below to it. Write that change down and state your new lab idea in the space below. Do that with three more changes.

Heat it	Freeze it	Reverse it	Double it
Bend it	Invert it	Poison it	Dehydrate it
Drown it	Stretch it	Fold it	Ignite it
Split it	Irradiate it	Oxidize it	Reduce it
Chill it	Speed it up	Color it	Grease it
Expand it	Substitute it	Remove it	Slow it down

    i. _____

_____

_____

_____

ii. _____

_____

_____

_____

iii. _____

_____

_____

_____

iv. _____

_____ STRETCHING!

_____

_____

Step Four • Create an Original Idea—Your Hypothesis
Your hypothesis should be stated as an opinion. You've done
the basic experiment, you've made observations, you're not stupid.
Put two and two together and make a PREDICTION. Be sure that you
are experimenting with just a single variable.

A. State your hypothesis in the space below. List the variable.
i. _____

_____

_____

_____

ii. Variable tested: _____

Sample Hypothesis Worksheet

On the previous two pages is a worksheet that will help you develop your thoughts and a hypothesis. Here is sample of the finished product to help you understand how to use it.

A. Write down the lab idea that you want to mutilate.
A mirror is placed in a tub of water. A beam of light is focused through the water onto the mirror, producing a rainbow on the wall.

B. List the possible variables you could change in the lab.
  i. **Source of light**
  ii. **The liquid in the tub**
  iii. **The distance from flashlight to mirror**

C. Take one variable listed in section B and apply one of the 24 changes to it. Write that change down and state your new lab idea in the space below.

The shape of the beam of light can be controlled by making and placing cardboard filters over the end of the flashlight. Various shapes such as circles, squares, and slits will produce different quality rainbows.

D. State your hypothesis in the space below. List the variable. Be sure that when you write the hypothesis, you are stating an idea and not asking a question.

Hypothesis: The narrower the beam of light, the tighter, brighter, and more focused the reflected rainbow will appear.

Variable tested: **The opening on the filter**

Scientific Method
• Step 2 •
Gather Information

Gather Information

Read about your topic and find out what we already know. Check books, videos, the Internet, and movies, talk with experts in the field, and molest an encyclopedia or two. Gather as much information as you can before you begin planning your experiment.

In particular, there are several things that you will want to pay special attention to and that should accompany any good science fair project.

A. Major Scientific Concepts

Be sure that you research and explain the main idea(s) that is / are driving your experiment. It may be a law of physics or chemical rule or an explanation of an aspect of plant physiology.

B. Scientific Words

As you use scientific terms in your paper, you should also define them in the margins of the paper or in a glossary at the end of the report. You cannot assume that everyone knows about geothermal energy transmutation in sulfur-loving bacterium. Be prepared to define some new terms for them. . . and scrub your hands really well when you are done if that is your project.

C. Historical Perspective

When did we first learn about this idea, and who is responsible for getting us this far? You need to give a historical perspective with names, dates, countries, awards, and other recognition.

Building a Research Foundation

1. This sheet is designed to help you organize your thoughts and give you some ideas on where to look for information on your topic. When you prepare your lab report, you will want to include the background information outlined below.

A. *Major Scientific Concepts (Two is plenty.)*

i. _____

_____

_____

_____

ii. _____

_____

_____

_____

B. *Scientific Words (No more than 10)*

i. _____

ii. _____

iii. _____

iv. _____

v. _____

vi. _____

vii. _____

viii. _____

ix. _____

x. _____

C. *Historical Perspective*
   Add this as you find it.

2. There are several sources of information that are available to help you fill in the details from the previous page.

A. *Contemporary Print Resources*
   (Magazines, Newspapers, Journals)

   i. _____
   ii. _____
   iii. _____
   iv. _____
   v. _____
   vi. _____

B. *Other Print Resources*
   (Books, Encyclopedias, Dictionaries, Textbooks)

   i. _____
   ii. _____
   iii. _____
   iv. _____
   v. _____
   vi. _____

C. *Celluloid Resources*
   (Films, Filmstrips, Videos)

   i. _____
   ii. _____
   iii. _____
   iv. _____
   v. _____
   vi. _____

D. *Electronic Resources*
   (Internet Website Addresses, DVDs, MP3s)

   i. _____

   ii. _____

   iii. _____

   iv. _____

   v. _____

   vi. _____

   vii. _____

   viii. _____

   ix. _____

   x. _____

E. *Human Resources*
   (Scientists, Engineers, Professionals, Professors, Teachers)

   i. _____

   ii. _____

   iii. _____

   iv. _____

   v. _____

   vi. _____

You may want to keep a record of all of your research and add it to the back of the report as an Appendix. Some teachers who are into volume think this is really cool. Others, like myself, find it a pain in the tuchus. No matter what you do, be sure to keep an accurate record of where you find data. If you quote from a report word for word, be sure to give proper credit with either a footnote or parenthetical reference. This is very important for credibility and accuracy. This will keep you out of trouble with plagiarism (copying without giving credit).

Scientific Method
• Step 3 •
Design Your Experiment

Acquire Your Lab Materials

The purpose of this section is to help you plan your experiment. You'll make a map of where you are going, how you want to get there, and what you will take along.

List the materials you will need to complete your experiment in the table below. Be sure to list multiples if you will need more than one item. Many science materials double as household items in their spare time. Check around the house before you buy anything from a science supply company or hardware store. For your convenience, we have listed some suppliers on page 21 of this book.

Material	Qty.	Source	$
1.			
2.			
3.			
4.			
5.			
6.			
7.			
8.			
9.			
10.			
11.			
12.			

Total $_____

Outline Your Experiment

This sheet is designed to help you outline your experiment. If you need more space, make a copy of this page to finish your outline. When you are done with this sheet, review it with an adult, make any necessary changes, review safety concerns on the next page, prepare your data tables, gather your equipment, and start to experiment.

In the space below, list what you are going to do in the order you are going to do it.

i. _____

_____

_____

_____

ii. _____

_____

_____

_____

iii. _____

_____

_____

_____

iv. _____

_____

_____

_____

v. _____

_____

_____

_____

Evaluate Safety Concerns

We have included an overall safety section in the front of this book on pages 18–20, but there are some very specific questions you need to ask, and prepare for, depending on the needs of your experiment. If you find that you need to prepare for any of these safety concerns, place a check mark next to the letter.

_____ A. *Goggles & Eyewash Station*

If you are mixing chemicals or working with materials that might splinter or produce flying objects, goggles and an eyewash station or sink with running water should be available.

_____ B. *Ventilation*

If you are mixing chemicals that could produce fire, smoke, fumes, or obnoxious odors, you will need to use a vented hood or go outside and perform the experiment in the fresh air.

_____ C. *Fire Blanket or Fire Extinguisher*

If you are working with potentially combustible chemicals or electricity, a fire blanket and extinguisher nearby are a must.

_____ D. *Chemical Disposal*

If your experiment produces a poisonous chemical or there are chemical-filled tissues (as in dissected animals), you may need to make arrangements to dispose of the by-products from your lab.

_____ E. *Electricity*

If you are working with materials and developing an idea that uses electricity, make sure that the wires are in good repair, that the electrical demand does not exceed the capacity of the supply, and that your work area is grounded.

_____ F. *Emergency Phone Numbers*

Look up and record the following phone numbers for the Fire Department: _____ , Poison Control: _____ , and Hospital: _____. Post them in an easy-to-find location.

Prepare Data Tables

Finally, you will want to prepare your data tables and have them ready to go before you start your experiment. Each data table should be easy to understand and easy for you to use.

A good data table has a **title** that describes the information being collected, and it identifies the **variable** and the **unit** being collected on each data line. The variable is *what* you are measuring and the unit is *how* you are measuring it. They are usually written like this:

Variable (unit), or to give you some examples:

Time (seconds)
Distance (meters)
Electricity (volts)

An example of a well-prepared data table looks like the sample below. We've cut the data table into thirds because the book is too small to display the whole line.

Determining the Boiling Point of Compound X_1

Time (min.)	0	1	2	3	4	5	6
Temp. (°C)							

Time (min.)	7	8	9	10	11	12	13
Temp. (°C)							

Time (min.)	14	15	16	17	18	19	20
Temp. (°C)							

Scientific Method
• Step 4 •
Conduct the Experiment

Lab Time

It's time to get going. You've generated a hypothesis, collected the materials, written out the procedure, checked the safety issues, and prepared your data tables. Fire it up. Here's the short list of things to remember as you experiment.

_____ A. *Follow the Procedure, Record Any Changes*

Follow your own directions specifically as you wrote them. If you find the need to change the procedure once you are into the experiment, that's fine; it's part of the process. Make sure to keep detailed records of the changes. When you repeat the experiment a second or third time, follow the new directions exactly.

_____ B. *Observe Safety Rules*

It's easier to complete the lab activity if you are in the lab rather than the emergency room.

_____ C. *Record Data Immediately*

Collect temperatures, distances, voltages, revolutions, and any other variables and immediately record them into your data table. Do not think you will be able to remember them and fill everything in after the lab is completed.

_____ D. *Repeat the Experiment Several Times*

The more data that you collect, the better. It will give you a larger data base and your averages are more meaningful. As you do multiple experiments, be sure to identify each data set by date and time so you can separate them out.

_____ E. *Prepare for Extended Experiments*

Some experiments require days or weeks to complete, particularly those with plants and animals or the growing of crystals. Prepare a safe place for your materials so your experiment can continue undisturbed while you collect the data. Be sure you've allowed enough time for your due date.

Scientific Method
• Step 5 •
Collect and Display Data

Types of Graphs

This section will give you some ideas on how you can display the information you are going to collect as a graph. A graph is simply a picture of the data that you gathered portrayed in a manner that is quick and easy to reference. There are four kinds of graphs described on the next two pages. If you find you need a leg up in the graphing department, we have a book in the series called *Data Tables & Graphing*. It will guide you through the process.

Line and Bar Graphs

These are the most common kinds of graphs. The most consistent variable is plotted on the "x", or horizontal, axis and the more temperamental variable is plotted along the "y", or vertical, axis. Each data point on a line graph is recorded as a dot on the graph and then all of the dots are connected to form a picture of the data. A bar graph starts on the horizontal axis and moves up to the data line.

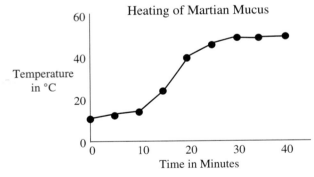

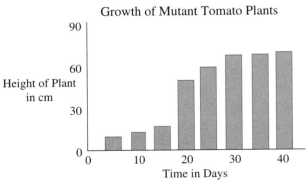

Best Fit Graphs

A best fit graph was created to show averages or trends rather than specific data points. The data that has been collected is plotted on a graph just as on a line graph, but instead of drawing a line from point to point to point, which sometimes is impossible anyway, you just free hand a line that hits "most of the data."

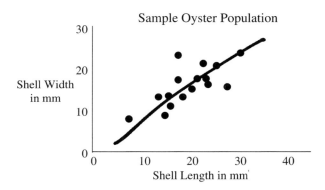

Pie Graphs

Pie graphs are used to show relationships between different groups. All of the data is totaled up and a percentage is determined for each group. The pie is then divided to show the relationship of one group to another.

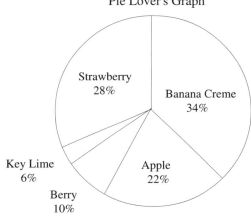

Other Kinds of Data

1. Written Notes & Observations

This is the age-old technique used by all scientists. Record your observations in a lab book. Written notes can be made quickly as the experiment is proceeding, and they can then be expounded upon later. Quite often notes made in the heat of an experiment are revisited during the evaluation portion of the process, and they can shed valuable light on how or why the experiment went the way it did.

2. Drawings

Quick sketches as well as fully developed drawings can be used as a way to report data for a science experiment. Be sure to title each drawing and, if possible, label what it is that you are looking at. Drawings that are actual size are best.

3. Photographs, Videotapes, and Audiotapes

Usually better than drawings, quicker, and more accurate, but you do have the added expense and time of developing the film. However, they can often capture images and details that are not usually seen by the naked eye.

4. The Experiment Itself

Some of the best data you can collect and present is the actual experiment itself. Nothing will speak more effectively for you than the plants you grew, the specimens you collected, or that big pile of tissue that was an armadillo you peeled from the tread of an 18-wheeler.

Scientific Method
• Step 6 •
Present Your Ideas

Oral Report Checklist

It is entirely possible that you will be asked to make an oral presentation to your classmates. This will give you an opportunity to explain what you did and how you did it. Quite often this presentation is part of your overall score, so if you do well, it will enhance your chances for one of the bigger awards.

To prepare for your oral report, your science fair presentation should include the following components:

Physical Display

_____a.   freestanding display board
                       hypothesis
                       data tables, graphs, photos, etc.
                       abstract (short summary)
_____b.   actual lab setup (equipment)

Oral Report

_____a.   hypothesis or question
_____b.   background information
                       concepts
                       word definitions
                       history or scientists
_____c.   experimental procedure
_____d.   data collected
                       data tables
                       graphs
                       photos or drawings
_____e.   conclusions and findings
_____f.   ask for questions

Set the display board up next to you on the table. Transfer the essential information to index cards. Use the index cards for reference, but do not read from them. Speak in a clear voice, hold your head up, and make eye contact with your peers. Ask if there are any questions before you finish and sit down.

Written Report Checklist

Next up is the written report, also called your lab write-up. After you compile or sort the data you have collected during the experiment and evaluate the results, you will be able to come to a conclusion about your hypothesis. Remember, disproving an idea is as valuable as proving it.

This sheet is designed to help you write up your science fair project and present your data in an organized manner. This is a final checklist for you.

To prepare your write-up, your science fair report should include the following components:

_____ a.   binder
_____ b.   cover page, title, & your name
_____ c.   abstract (one paragraph summary)
_____ d.   table of contents with page numbers
_____ e.   hypothesis or question
_____ f.   background information
                        concepts
                        word definitions
                        history or scientists
_____ g.   list of materials used
_____ h.   experimental procedure
                        written description
                        photo or drawing of setup
_____ i.   data collected
                        data tables
                        graphs
                        photos or drawings
_____ j.   conclusions and findings
_____ k.   glossary of terms
_____ l.   references

Display Checklist

Prepare your display to accompany the report. A good display should include the following:

Freestanding Display

_____ a.   freestanding cardboard back
_____ b.   title of experiment
_____ c.   your name
_____ d.   hypothesis
_____ e.   findings of the experiment
_____ f.   photo or illustrations of equipment
_____ g.   data tables or graphs

Additional Display Items

_____ h.   a copy of the write-up
_____ i.   actual lab equipment setup

Index

Index

Index

Index

Notes

More Science Books

Catch a Wave

50 hands-on lab activities that sound off on the topic of noise, vibration, waves, the Doppler effect, and associated ideas.

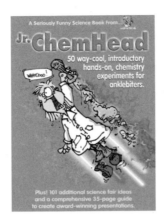

Jr. Chemhead

50 hands-on lab activities that delve into the world of chemistry and the characteristics of atoms, molecules, and other basic chemistry ideas.

Newton Take 3

50 hands-on lab activities that explore the world of mechanics, forces, gravity, and Newton's three laws of motion.

Photon U

50 hands-on lab activities from the world of light. Starts with the basic colors of the rainbow and works you way up to polarizing filters and UV light.

Electron Herding 101

50 hands-on lab activities that introduce static electricity, circuit electricity, and include a number of fun and very easy-to-build projects.

Opposites Attract

50 hands-on lab activities that delve into the world of natural and man-made magnets as well as the characteristics of magnetic attraction.